THE
DUNE'S
TWISTED
EDGE

THE
DUNE'S
TWISTED
EDGE

Journeys
in the
Levant

Gabriel
Levin

THE UNIVERSITY OF CHICAGO PRESS

CHICAGO AND LONDON

GABRIEL LEVIN is the author of four books of poems, most recently *To These Dark Steps*, and has published several collections in translation. He lives in Jerusalem.

The University of Chicago Press, Chicago 60637
The University of Chicago Press, Ltd., London
© 2013 by The University of Chicago
All rights reserved. Published 2013.
Printed in the United States of America

Grateful acknowledgment is made to the *Chicago Review*, *Parnassus*, *Raritan*, and *Trafika*, where these essays have previously appeared in modified form. "Hezekiah's Tunnel" appeared in a small-book format with Ibis Editions (1997) and was republished, along with "Attir" and "Notes from Wadi Rumm," in a French edition as *Le Tunnel D'Ézéchias* by Le Bruit du Temps (2010). "Attir" appeared in a limited-edition format as *Pleasant if Somewhat Rude Views*, photos by Mikael Levin (Paris: onestar press, 2005).

22 21 20 19 18 17 16 15 14 13   1 2 3 4 5

ISBN-13: 978-0-226-92367-3 (cloth)
ISBN-13: 978-0-226-92368-0 (e-book)
ISBN-10: 0-226-92367-3 (cloth)
ISBN-10: 0-226-92368-1 (e-book)

Library of Congress Cataloging-in-Publication Data

Levin, Gabriel, 1948– author.
    [Essays. Selections. 2012]
    The dune's twisted edge : journey in the Levant / Gabriel Levin.
      pages   cm.
    Collection of previously published essays.
    Includes bibliographical references.
    ISBN-13: 978-0-226-92367-3 (hardcover : alkaline paper)
    ISBN-10: 0-226-92367-3 (hardcover : alkaline paper)
    ISBN-13: 978-0-226-92368-0 (e-book)
    ISBN-10: 0-226-92368-1 (e-book)   1. Essays. 2. Middle Eastern poetry 3. Middle East—Description and travel. 4. Middle Easterners. I. Levin, Gabriel, 1948– Seeking a poetics of the Fertile Crescent. Contains (work):   II. Levin, Gabriel, 1948– Hezekiah's tunnel. Contains (work):   III. Levin, Gabriel, 1948– Who keened over the bones of dead encampments. Contains (work):   IV. Levin, Gabriel, 1948– Notes from Wadi Rumm. Contains (work):   V. Levin, Gabriel, 1948– Galilean centos. Contains (work):   VI. Title.
    PR9510.9L48A6 2012
    824'.914—dc23

2012009843

♾ This paper meets the requirements of ANSI/NISO Z39.48-1992 (Permanence of Paper).

Contents

All Things Levantine

How to speak of the imaginative reach of a land habitually seen as a seedbed of faiths and heresies, confluences and ruptures—a vast Debatable Ground, in the words of one traveling Scottish theologian writing at the end of the nineteenth century—trouble spot and findspot, ruin and renewal, fault line and ragged clime, with a medley of people and languages once known with mingled affection and wariness as Levantine? The appellation crops up repeatedly in the journals of travel writers, orientalists, merchants, and adventurers of one sort or another visiting the eastern shores of the Mediterranean in the eighteenth and nineteenth centuries. But in my mind the term *Levant*, which can also mean an easterly wind and, in French, the rising sun, blended smoothly with a line toward the end of Paul Valéry's "Le Cimetière Marin": "Le vent se lève! . . . Il faut tenter de vivre!" wherein the French *levant* and *le vent* are homophonic. In my imagination, then, the wind, the sunrise, and the Levant were all one and the same, as was the exhortation to make something of my life.

Writing would become synonymous with discovering or rather repeatedly reinventing myself as a roving free agent in the Middle East, nourished by its layers of myths, its diverse folklores, and its ancient as well as modern poetic traditions. This required some travel, especially to the more arid parts of the region—which have been a constant source of inspiration for me, perhaps because of the fleeting yet tenacious hold on life of its flora and fauna—and a great deal of stay-at-home rummaging in old books and lexicons, travelogues, field guides, and language manuals.

Why I should have felt a need to seek out the hybrid and the syncretic in a country of avowed national and religious orthodoxies, at least in the last century, may be partly understood by my own complete lack of ideological baggage upon landing in Haifa in 1972. My girlfriend and I had arrived by ferry from Venice with our bicycles in its hold. That same afternoon a train bore us and our bikes and saddlebags to Jerusalem, where I planned to pursue graduate studies at the Hebrew University for a year, at most two. I was, like so many of my generation, at loose ends after completing my undergraduate studies, and by coming to Israel I was living out, or perhaps completing, what was popularly called an extended moratorium. We may have been chugging up the hills to Jerusalem, but I was definitely not an *oleh*, or new immigrant, with its connotations of ascending and arrival at one's longed-for destination, Eretz Yisrael. Instead I saw myself—and here lies the first compound identity—as part tourist, part student, and, having lived with my family in a small village north of Tel Aviv between 1958 and 1967, part prodigal son.

I had picked up some Hebrew in the elementary school I attended for two years before cajoling my parents into sending me to the newly established American International School in Kfar Shmaryahu. In the end they consented, as they would with my younger brother and my sister, although my sister would end up in the French school run by les soeurs de Saint-Joseph in old Jaffa. We were definitely not adjusting to the Zionist dream, which was odd, as my father had arrived in Palestine as a young man in 1925. He had reported on the opening of the Hebrew University on Mount Scopus and in 1931 had even published *Yehuda*, a novel in English on kibbutz life. He was without question an ardent Zionist of the old socialist school; in 1947, in the wake of World War II, he would infect my French mother with his enthusiasm for the state-in-the-making as they set out together to film the illegal immigration to Palestine of Jewish survivors from the concentration camps.

But things would change once Israel gained statehood, and we children must have sensed our parents' unease as we kept moving from one coastal town to another in the years preceding the Six-Day War. The move from New York had been at my mother's instigation and was primarily motivated by her own difficulty in adjusting to the United States and her desire to distance my father from a prolonged, crippling legal battle he had been waging. There was, even in those days, the Israel Cure: a dream of sun-drenched Mediterranean rejuvenation, sustained by my parents' memories—a heady mix of romance and high adventure—of Mandate Palestine and the small, idealistic community of *yishuv* (settlement) Jews they had encountered there.

There existed, as far as I can see, two major reasons for my parents' inability to acclimatize, the first religious and the second political. My mother's parents had converted to Catholicism shortly after the end of World War I, and in essence she had been brought up as a Catholic Jew. The orthodox rabbinate controlled practically all aspects of civic life in Israel, and it did not take long for my parents to find out that her family's history had been filed away in the Ministry of Interior's infamous "black book" of renegade Jews. This was taken by my parents with a mixture of revulsion, good humor, and, on my mother's part, even pride, imagining herself as an agent provocateur in the eyes of the fledgling nation-state—but the gradual dawning in their minds of the predicament of the Palestinian population in Israel was a different matter.

There prevailed at the time an eerie, palpable silence concerning the Arab villagers and townspeople who hadn't fled or been expelled during the Arab-Israeli War of 1948 and its aftermath, a community that had shrunk from close to a million inhabitants to 180,000 and which remained, though granted citizenship in 1950, under a military government until 1966. Arab citizens needed special permits to travel from their own villages or towns, they were subject to curfews, and their freedom of speech had been severely curtailed: all articles, books, stories, and poems slated for publication in Arabic were submitted to a military censor. The fifties was a period of massive absorption of immigrants, wherein the wave of survivors from Europe's concentration camps had been followed by an even greater wave of Jewish refugees from Iraq, Yemen, Iran, and North Africa. Immigrants to the new agricultural settlements — *moshavim* — in the Galilee chose either to blithely ignore their Palestinian neighbors or to justify on moral grounds their occupying and tilling plots that were, for the most part, confiscated Arab-owned lands: hadn't they (in numbers, some 700,000, almost equal to the Palestinians') been traumatized and uprooted from their homes as well?

Thus soon after we moved into a rented house in the coastal town of Bet Yanai in 1958, my father was offered a home in Ein Hod, formerly Ein Hawd, which had been converted into an artist village by Dadaist painter Marcel Yanco.[1] My father firmly refused. Soon afterward he would acquire for his own use a one-room, barrel-vaulted hut built by the British that had been used as a cliff-side lookout against the same illegal ships he had filmed in 1947. This pleased him far better.

To speak of what had happened to the Arab population was taboo. There were exceptions of course, such as S. Yizhar's remarkable novella of 1949, *Khirbet Khizeh*, and the publication three years later of Avot Yeshurun's controversial poem "Pesach al kuchim" (Passover on caves), which drew parallels between the Palestinian expulsion and the Holocaust. To mention the "Arab problem" was inviting the return of the repressed, and it now seems highly unusual that in the sixties my parents should have regularly attended the first Arab-Jewish dialogue group in Israel. Hosted by Nina Denur in her home in Haifa, it consisted of a small band of left-leaning Jewish and Arab intellectuals and writers. (Denur also happened to be the wife of Holocaust survivor Ka-Tzetnik, who in his testimony during the Eichmann trial had spoken dramatically of "planet Auschwitz" before slumping over and losing consciousness.) It was there that my parents met and befriended Rashid Hussein, the legendary Palestinian poet from the Galilean village of Musmus, who had—as the great exception to the rule—moved to Tel Aviv in 1958 to write for and edit the Arab-language magazine *al-Fajr*, published by Mapam, the Israeli Socialist Zionist party.[2]

We lived, so it seemed, in a strange, extraterritorial zone, neither tourists nor full citizens—my parents would in fact eventually acquire temporary resident status. We never learned the language properly, and my parents mixed with the bohemia of Tel Aviv and the foreign diplomats, journalists, writers, and artists passing through the country; for us, Israel was in many ways more of an extended holiday than a place in which to put down roots. And although my parents did finally build a home overlooking the Mediterranean in the midsixties, we remained constantly on the move. The holiday ended in 1967. Most of the students at the American International School, those whose parents were attached to the diplomatic corps, had been airlifted to Rome weeks before the onset of the Six-Day War, and with the school shut down, my high-school graduation canceled (which I recall dreading far more than the impending war), I spent a good deal of my time digging and sandbagging trenches in people's yards. My parents and my sister—she had been studying journalism in Paris—would report on the war. I'm not sure they were assigned to any specific newspaper, however, as my mother had simply stuck on the windshield of our Renault a card from a laundry press on which she'd removed the word *laundry*. By September we returned to New York, and I started my freshman year in college. My parents would return to their home in Herzliya-on-Sea in 1969 and again in the early seventies, but otherwise their sojourns became increasingly sporadic, with my father occasionally flying in on his own to work in his concrete Mandate hut on the seaside cliff in Bet Yanai. The country, with its occupied lands, its Messianic settlement movement, and the surging power of its ultra-Orthodox communities, had lost its appeal.

It is no small wonder, then, that I should have dithered upon arriving in Jerusalem in 1972. I too kept extending my student and temporary resident status for a good ten years before acquiring citizenship, and even when the clerk at the Ministry of Interior did finally hand me my identity card, he insisted on writing "France" for my religion (or *leom*, "nation," in Hebrew). Having informed me that I wasn't Jewish—my mother's bulging file took up a corner of his desk—he had wanted to know what religion to write on the dotted line: Christian? I shook my head. Muslim? Again I said no. Just leave it blank, I said. I can't do that, he answered. Where were you born? In Paris. Okay, I'll write down "France."

In the mideighties, shortly after becoming, willy-nilly, an Israeli citizen, I was by chance given the opportunity to translate a novella by S. Y. Agnon in which the young narrator, Tirza, is tutored in her home in Polish Galicia by both a *melamed*—an instructor of traditional Jewish subjects—and a Hebrew teacher. The two are constantly picking at each other, and before long it becomes clear that the *melamed* and the teacher stand for the two dominant forces, traditional and progressive, vying for the hearts of young Jews in eastern Europe. The novella was written in 1921, when the use of the term *ivri*, Hebrew, a biblical appellation for the people of Israel, was commonly adopted by secular Zionists in distinguishing themselves from the shtetl Jew. *Ivri* became synonymous with the *chalutz*, or pioneer spirit, of the new Jew tilling the land or paving roads in Palestine—bold, irreverent, scorning the old ways.

The squabbling between the *melamed* and the Hebrew teacher was, then, a familiar scene within the burgeoning Zionist movement itself, which was roughly split in two: the ingatherers[3] and the outlanders, the purifiers of the tribe and the diversifiers seeking other traditions that might nourish their own. Thus in the early days of modern Hebrew letters there was Bialik and Tchernikovsky, Agnon and Brenner. I admired Bialik, but I *dug* Tchernikovsky; the former, I was ready to admit, might have been a better poet, whose words swept clean the "cobwebs of the heart";[4] but the latter was eclectic in his tastes and embraced in his verse and numerous translations a vision of a rejuvenated Hebrew soul rooted in the heterodox, pagan cultures of the Fertile Crescent. "I was to my god like a hyacinth or mallow," opens his corona sonnet "To the Sun," a cycle teeming with allusions to Greek and Chaldean mythology yet formally indebted to both the Italian Renaissance and the Russian symbolists who had revived the form toward the end of the nineteenth century.[5]

Since I was not, according to the Ministry of Interior, exactly kosher as a Jew, I could at least think of myself as an *ivri*, which in my mind was tinged with romantic overtones as the *ivri* sought to rediscover the self in the geographical and cultural strata of the old/new Semitic Near East. So, too, traces of Middle Eastern primitive myths could be found in the Old Testament: Akkadian, Ugarit, Canaanite, Egyptian, Phoenician, Greek. And hadn't the high modernist been fascinated with the primitive as well? One had only to think of Picasso's *Les Demoiselles d'Avignon*; Stravinsky's *Rites of Spring*; and Charles Olson's *Maximus Poems*, a double leaf of which I had tacked to the closet in my father's hut after his death, which begins, "I have had to learn the simplest things / last. Which made for difficulties."

And locally there was the poetry and polemical writings of Yonatan Ratosh, who in Tel Aviv during the forties and fifties had developed his own Canaanite myth as an answer to European

Jewry.[6] The doctrine—which called for a rejection of the Diaspora altogether and the refashioning of the Israeli as a Canaanite, namely as a reborn Semite bound to autochthonous gods of yore— was a bit much, but its aesthetic dimensions did fire the imagination of a host of native Israeli writers and artists. Among those was Yitzhak Danziger, whose statue in red Nubian sandstone of Nimrod the hunter, naked, uncircumcised, with a hawk perched on his shoulder, would achieve iconic status. Danziger was to Ratosh what Gaudier-Brzeska had been to Pound. "The HAMITE VORTEX of Egypt, the land of plenty," Gaudier-Brzeska had written in his "Vortex" manifesto of 1914, while Pound spoke of the young sculptor's faculty for synthesis, all of which is reechoed in Danziger's and Ratosh's probing of the archaic world of the Near East. Back in the seventies, when I first set eyes on *Nimrod*, I had no idea that its creator was the same person who had acted as Avram, the dark, lean kibbutznik, the *ivri* and adoptive father of a child Holocaust survivor in *My Father's House*, a feature film written and produced by my father in Palestine in 1946.[7] Nor did I realize that a frequent visitor to our home, Jacqueline Kahanoff, a Cairene Jew, novelist, and author of short, pristine essays—in English—of Levantine life in Egypt between the wars, had been discovered at the time by the Canaanites and published in Hebrew translation in their literary magazine, *Keshet*. She would, in fact, be credited by her Israeli contemporaries with using *Levantinism* as a positive, composite term in speaking of the melding of Eastern and the Western traits in Israeli society.[8]

So there were the purifiers and the diversifiers. And as my travels extended down the Red Sea to Egypt, across the Dead Sea into Jordan, and along the eastern basin of the Mediterranean, more got thrown into the mix—Hellene, Roman, Nabatean, Byzantine, Bedouin, an amalgam that would make, in Dennis Silk's words, for a "stinky Levant egg . . . all garlic and hope." And it was indeed *The Punished Land*, published in 1980 by the London-born poet, that first alerted me to the possibilities of working within a broader, syncretic tradition of manifold selves wherein I might court the foreign, the disparate and anomalous. Could one be at once a Hellene and a Hebrew? Might one be lured by the likes of Walid Ibn Yazid *and* the half-crazed Noah Stern? "Hezekiah's Tunnel," the earliest essay in this collection, was in effect my first attempt at broaching simultaneously two fractured narratives—Hebrew and Arab—using the technique of montage, though by the time I finished writing it I understood that I was, in a fashion, chasing after the elusive convolutions of the arabesque.

But the literary encounter soon gave way to the real-life encounter, or rather one would evoke the other as I ventured south—coming into contact with the Bedouin of the Negev and of Wadi Rumm in south Jordan—as well as north into the Arab villages of the Galilee. "Art makes for distance from the I. Art requires that we travel a certain space in a certain direction, on a certain road." These words from Paul Celan's essay "The Meridian" have stood me in good stead, "for the sake of an encounter."[9] Were not the poet Taha Muhammad Ali—with whom I regularly met in Nazareth during my first jabs at translating a handful of his compositions into English—Sulciman ben Musa of the unrecognized Bedouin village of Attir, and Fathi Halileh part of an ongoing, vital, or perhaps I should say, in deference to Celan, *desperate* conversation, as much with myself as with my interlocutors and, by extension, with Israel and its downward-spiraling relations vis-à-vis its own Palestinian minority? Each in his own way had lent a guiding hand as I plodded along. As it turned out, I would soon hear from Taha Muhammad Ali that back in the fifties and sixties he had entertained in his souvenir shop on Casanova Street my parents' old friend Rashid Hussein. Seated on Taha's balcony overlooking his plot of fruit trees—which always made me think of Sir Thomas Browne's remarkable meditation on quintuple plantations in *The Garden of Cyrus* (had Browne caught wind of the arabesque during his medical studies in Montpellier?)—while he pantomimed the meaning of certain words in his poems, I was beginning to feel that my own choices had been determined a long time ago.

And yet politics would rarely come up. What I hope will be made clear in these essays is that all such encounters, whether short-lived or prolonged, sporadic or lasting, were registered on the skin, so to speak, as immediate sense impressions, sensitized as never before and tested as qualities of attention. Apprehending reality at close quarters, whether wandering in Wadi Rumm or dipping into the hot baths at Hamat Gader, strangeness was welcomed, even courted as the necessary "distance from the I" in which to see the world afresh. Perhaps this is what Victor Segalen meant when he wrote of exoticism as "a fundamental Law of the Intensity of *Sensation*, of the exaltation of Feeling; and therefore of living."[10]

Exoticism, not unlike orientalism, has received a bad name in our own times; among other offenses it is generally considered to be one more manifestation of the West's postcolonial misrepresentation of the East. This may often be the case, but I would like to believe that it is not axiomatic, and that its very challenge of diversity has posited all along—to quote Segalen again—"the ability to *conceive otherwise.*"[11] Thus the pre-Islamic poets would grant me an aperture into a synergetic world of plenitude in the midst of scarcity, and in my own desert jaunts the *qasida* served not only as a field guide—al-Qays, in describing his latest conquest, compares her waist to a camel's nose ring, while her shinbone is "lean as the stalk of a papyrus" and her fingers are "soft as the sand worms of Zaby, or tamarisk toothpicks"[12]—but as a running testimony of Otherwise for both ingatherers and outlanders. And, as with all things Levantine, what first appeared as two distinct categories converged into a unified ethos of contrary inclinations.

Seeking a Poetics
of the Fertile Crescent

The Fertile Crescent sweeps across the eastern shoreline of the Mediterranean and down to Egypt, then stretches inland into the desert wastes of modern-day Iraq. That's a large enough area to host a conglomeration of myths and oral traditions, each with its own aesthetics. Here I would like to describe three literary models, three ancient paradigmatic forms—the *katabasis*, the *qasida*, and the arabesque—that appear to have emerged from specific topologies or ground conditions of a region that has served as a conduit between the East and the West for thousands of years.

But why a poetics in the first place? Do we really need yet another literary model? Might it not be best to simply "go on your nerve," as Frank O'Hara wrote in "Personism: A Manifesto"? "If someone's chasing you down the street with a knife you just run."[1] O'Hara was constantly looking for ways to outwit his own habits of thought; his spontaneity, his own "kinetic discharges" and indeterminacies, not only were a part of the poetics of his time and place but may have originated, albeit unknowingly, in one of the models I will be discussing here. But I am getting ahead of myself. Why a poetics then? Or rather, why seek a poetics? It is the pursuit here that counts, and in effect the three topographical models I will be introducing share a common rule: they are all on the move. It follows that the region's vast, shifting sands and the sort of nomadic existence it fostered would leave an imprint on its poetry. To inscribe is to possess and be possessed by the land. Perhaps this is what D. H. Lawrence meant in speaking of Walt Whitman: "The soul living her life along the incarnate mystery of the open road."[2] The mystery of the journey here encompasses both the ancientness of the three topologies in their Eastern dress as well as their relocated Western guise in our own times. We inscribe and are inscribed by traces of all three landforms in the sprawl of our own urban scapes, in our thoroughfares, tentacular suburbs, and straggle of strip malls—locus of the modern imagination.

Ever since the biblical injunction to Abraham, "Get thee out of thy country,"[3] caravans have crossed and recrossed the Fertile Crescent. Step out into the desert and you can still find traces of temporary habitation, way stations, watering holes, the rutted remains of the ancient spice trade route and the Roman King's Highway. The marvel is that so many people have tramped through these barren grounds. There were, to name a few, Canaanites and Hittites, Jebusites, Hebrews and Mesopotamians, Egyptians and Arabians, Phoenicians, Philistines, Persians, Greeks and Romans, Nabateans, Byzantines, Muslims, Franks and Ottomans, Mameluks, Circassians, and closer to our own times, Palestinians, Druze, Jews, Armenians, Germans, Italians, French, and British. These were nomads and farmers, seafarers and caravanners, slaves and freemen, merchants and mercenaries, colonists and zealots. Some drove their neighbors out, while others took on their dress and customs. All ensured that the flow of goods between Asia and Europe continued to run through their territory. Household gods were swapped on the sly like choice marbles, divine names reshuffled and duplicated in the heavens—at least until the Israelites trekked out of Sinai with the brainteaser

I AM THAT I AM (Ehyeh-Asher-Ehyeh), or, in another rendition, I WILL BE WHAT I WILL BE.

Predating the Sinaic theophany by a millennia, however, are the Sumerian tales of the goddess Inanna, inscribed in cuneiform on clay tablets. And it is specifically in "The Descent of Inanna" that we witness the very first description of a *katabasis*, or downward-spiraling voyage into the Great Below. Inanna's journey begins by the awakening of her auditory faculty, for the word *ear* in Sumerian also stands for wisdom: "From the Great Above she opened her ear to the Great Below."[4] What follows is a narrative of descent, bodily fragmentation, rescue, substitution, self-transformation (common to so many myths), and slow re-ascent: Inanna is stripped of her clothes and jewels as she passes through the seven gates of the underworld; struck by her envious sister Ereshkigal, ruler of the underworld, she is "turned into a corpse, / a piece of rotting meat, / and hung from a hook on the wall," until rescued and reanimated from the Great Below by her faithful servant, Ninshubur.[5] There is an endearing scene after Inanna's husband, Dumuzi—otherwise known to us as the seasonal vegetation god Tammuz—has been sacrificed in her stead, and it is now his sister's turn to seek out her brother and raise him from the dead. Here is how Dumuzi's whereabouts are discovered:

When Inanna saw the grief of Geshtinanna,
She spoke to her gently:
"Your brother's house is no more.
Dumuzi has been carried away by the *galla*.
I would take you to him,
But I do not know the place."

Then a fly appeared.
The holy fly circled the air above Inanna's head and spoke:

"If I tell you where Dumuzi is,
What will you give me?"

Inanna said:
"If you tell me,
I will let you frequent the beer-houses and taverns.
I will let you dwell among the talk of the wise ones.
I will let you dwell among the songs of the minstrels."

The fly spoke:
"Lift your eyes to the edges of the steppe,
Lift your eyes to Arali.
There you will find Geshtinanna's brother,
There you will find the shepherd Dumuzi."[6]

The common fly, the little fly brushed away several millennia later by Blake's "thoughtless hand," acquires newfound relevance in divulging its secret. Henceforth it too will play a part in the life of ancient society, privy, like the proverbial "fly on the wall," to the talk and song of taverns. This is a wonderfully telling detail, at once fantastical and partaking of a certain inner psychological truth. It recalls a similar juxtaposition in an early Sumerian version of the *Epic of Gilgamesh*. In this version, known as Tablet 12, Gilgamesh, the shepherd-king of the city of Uruk and Inanna's earthly brother, is seen playing with a stick and ball, carried piggyback by the orphans of Uruk. When the orphans complain to the gods, the ball falls into the netherworld, and Enkidu, Gilgamesh's trusted companion, volunteers to retrieve it. So begins another great descent as Gilgamesh warns his friend of the dangers of his journey:

If today you descend to the underworld,
Let me give you advice, may you heed my advice,

I will have a word with you, may you pay attention to it.
Do not put on clean clothes,
They would surely see it as the sign of a stranger.
Do not anoint yourself with fine oil from a jar,
They would surely encircle you when they smell it.
Do not hurl your throw stick in the netherworld,
Those killed by a throw stick would surely encircle you.
Do not take up your staff in the netherworld,
The ghosts would surely hover around you.
Do not put shoes on your feet,
The netherworld would surely raise a clamor.
Do not kiss your wife you loved,
Do not strike your son you hated,
The pleas of the netherworld would surely seize you.
The one who lies there, the one who lies there,
The mother of the god Ninazu who lies there,
Her radiant shoulders are not clothed,
On her radiant bosom no linen garment is spread.
She clatters her fingernails like a drum,
She rips out her hair like leeks.[7]

Enkidu ignores his friend's advice. Like a stubborn child, he
does exactly what he was told not to do. He puts on clean clothes,
he anoints himself, he hurls his throw stick, and so on. He fails, in
other words, to blend in, safeguarding his soul for the re-ascent.
With Enkidu trapped in the underworld, Gilgamesh now scurries
from one god to another, begging their assistance in his effort to
bring Enkidu back to the light of day.

The *katabasis* in both cuneiform texts plummets down and
soars back up and out again as it plays its part—not altogether
malevolent—in the protagonist's journey of self-transformation.
The whimsy of such texts (tablets), the casual tone, and the very
physicality of the netherworld with its seven gates suggest that

the Sumerians and Akkadians had a real terrain in mind—geological fault lines such as the Syrian-African Rift that might yawn open at one's feet (as in the Gilgamesh tablet). These tales link both inner and outer realities. In our own times—post-Pound, post-Olson and Seferis, the great modern mythographers—such a journey will acquire a different, more blatantly intrapsychic coloration. Thus Seferis will write: "I woke with this marble head in my hands; / it exhausts my elbows and I don't know where to put it down. / It was falling into the dream as I was coming out of the dream / so our life became one and it will be very difficult for it to separate again."[8] And "harrowing Hell for a casket Proserpina keeps," Robert Duncan writes, in his retelling of the myth of Cupid and Psyche in "A Poem Beginning with a Line by Pindar":

                                    that must not
        be opened . . . containing beauty?
        no! Melancholy coild like a serpent
                                    that is deadly sleep
        we are not permitted
                    to succumb to.
        These are the old tasks.
        You've heard them before.[9]

These are the old tasks, suggesting vigilance and continuity, but also the near depletion of the belated. In the wake of *The Cantos*, is ascent possible? Surely descent and fragmentation, but renewal? How are we to read canto CXVI, "I have brought the great ball of crystal; / who can lift it? / Can you enter the great acorn of light?" followed by the palinode, "But the beauty is not the madness / Tho' my errors and wrecks lie about me, / And I am not a demigod, / I cannot make it cohere"?[10]

The constantly shifting terrain on which Pound stood—from the United States to London, France, Italy, St. Elizabeth (one could make a case for the madhouse being extraterritorial, a Poundian nodal point for the ingathering of cultural eclecticism), and finally to Venice—would in the end bottom out under the burden of memory, personal and collective: the crystal ball that shatters in the poet's downward journey through *The Cantos* and refuses to cohere.

*   *   *

A century earlier Herman Melville had traced a similar downward-spiraling journey, although in his case the descent was uniquely grounded in the East and inscribed in his journals, which depict a two-week sojourn in Ottoman Palestine in 1857. Melville was thirty-seven. In the span of twelve years (1845–57) he had written nine novels and a collection of short fiction. By all accounts he was suffering from exhaustion, chronic back pain and eyestrain, and despondency. The last was undoubtedly aggravated by the steady decline in his literary reputation. The voyage to Europe and the Middle East was financed by his father-in-law, who believed, along with his daughter, that travel might act as a tonic to Melville's declining spirits. Nathaniel Hawthorne hosted Melville in Liverpool on the outbound voyage, and recorded the visit in his journal. There he quoted Melville as saying that he had "pretty much made up his mind to be annihilated." Hawthorne also wrote, memorably, "He can neither believe, nor be comfortable in his unbelief; and he is too honest and courageous not to try to do one or the other."[11]

Clarel, Melville's late novel-in-verse set in Jerusalem and its environs, would prove the acuteness of Hawthorne's analysis. But before getting to *Clarel* and Melville's *katabasis*, I would like to consider the journal entries from his sojourn, where he records the slow, winding descent on horseback to the Dead Sea as well as the zigzag ascent back to Jerusalem via Mar Saba and Bethlehem.

These jottings will provide the topological groundwork for "The Wilderness," the second part of *Clarel*, which Melville set out to write in 1867, ten years after his journey to Palestine.

Where Kedron opens into the Plain of Jericho looks like Gate of Hell . . . foam on beach & pebbles like slaver of mad dog— smarting bitter of the water,—carried the bitter in my mouth all day—bitterness of life—thought of all bitter things—Bitter is it to be poor & bitter, to be reviled, & Oh bitter are these waters of Death, thought I. Rainbow over Dead Sea—heaven, after all, has no malice against it.—Old boughs tossed up by water—relics of pick-nick—nought to eat but bitumen & ashes with desert [*sic*] of Sodom apples washed down with water of Dead Sea. Must bring your own provisions, as well, too, for mind as body—for all is barren. Drank of brook, but brackish.—Ascended among the mountains again—barren.[12]

Here, then, are the ground conditions, recorded in a startling and startled shorthand, part literary romance and part testing ground for unmediated poetic speech. As to the former, Melville records in twelve compact pages his own bitter disappointment upon beholding the holy sites and the "diabolical landscapes"[13] stripped of romantic embellishments. In its most ancient mythic manifestations, the *katabasis* is primarily a form of divestment, a whittling down of the self and dispelling of the false, which is precisely what occurs in Melville's journals as he is confronted time and again with the "mere refuse & rubbish of creation."[14] And yet at the same time we witness on Melville's part an effort to reconstitute the self—he had written to Hawthorne in the early days of their friendship: "I feel that the Godhead is broken up like the bread at the Supper, and that we are the pieces"[15]—by an effortful, tentative testing of poetic speech.

A week after visiting Jerusalem and the Dead Sea, while waiting in Joppa (modern-day Jaffa) for his ship to set sail for Beirut, Melville writes, "*Wandering among the tombs*—till I began to think myself one of the possessed with devels [*sic*]."[16] His impressions are still fresh, but he crafts his words retrospectively: "In pursuance of my object, the saturation of my mind with the atmosphere of Jerusalem, offering myself up a passive subject, and no unwilling one, to its weird impressions, I always rose at dawn & walked without the walls."[17] And elsewhere, in a section titled "Barrenness of Judea," "Whitish mildew pervading whole tracts of landscape—bleached—leprosy—encrustation of curses—old cheese   bones of rocks,   crunched, knawed [*sic*], & mumbled."[18] Such hovering, seismic clauses will eventually reappear, slightly altered, in the grand design of Melville's 500-page, octosyllabic, 18,000-line philosophical novel-in-verse, "a metrical affair, a pilgrimage or what not . . . eminently adapted for unpopularity."[19] But I would propose that it is precisely in the journals that we may recognize the encoding of an original approach to a language—scribbled down hastily, impulsively, vividly—of bewilderment. Melville, on the open road, is possessed by the land; perhaps it is in the nature of the *katabasis* to take hold and—in time—to release the individual for the upward journey. In ancient times the "taking hold" and release was enacted by demonic forces, while Melville would be released, or at least reprieved, by the power of his own words. Dennis Silk, the English-born Jerusalemite and poet of the Levant par excellence, called this "dry souls working a language out, / making in limestone a mouth."[20]

Working a language out in "mineral silence" (to quote another of Silk's phrases) and in limestone would then turn into the protracted making of *Clarel*, begun in 1867 and finished some ten years later. The labor involved in its composition—Melville's wife, Lizzie, would call *Clarel* his "dreadful *incubus* of a book"[21]—

may have been the result of drastically altered circumstances: not only was Melville far removed from the landscape that had momentarily galvanized his attention, but his own life had undergone profound changes, including the sale of Arrowhead, his estate in Massachusetts; his increased anonymity; his moving with his family to New York City; his employment as a customs inspector on the Hudson River piers; and, critically, the suicide of his son Malcolm the very year he set out to write his narrative of spiritual crisis. *Clarel* was at least in part, as Andrew Delbanco suggests, "a work of mourning,"[22] enacting the Orpheus-like descent and failed retrieval of his beloved son, transformed in the poem into the nebulous figure of Ruth, the object of Clarel's idealized love, who dies of grief after her father is murdered: "O blind, blind, barren universe! / Now am I like a bough torn down, / And I must wither, cloud or sun!— / Had I been near, this had not been."[23]

Melville allegorizes his real if disorienting journey of January 1857 as a descent into the underworld by an eccentric crew of mostly disenchanted pilgrims, including Clarel, an American student "snatched from grace, / and waylaid in the holy place." Canto 11 of book 2, midway along the road winding down from Jerusalem to the Dead Sea, concludes:

> For Judah here—
> Let Erebus her rival own:
> 'Tis horror absolute—severe,
> Dead, livid, honey-combed, dumb, fell—
> A caked depopulated hell;
> Yet so created, judged by sense,
> And visaged in significance
> Of settled anger terrible.
> Profoundly cloven through the scene
> Winds Kedron—word (the scholar saith)
> Importing anguish hard on death.

And aptly may such named ravine
Conduct unto Lot's mortal Sea
In cleavage from Gethsemane
Where it begins.
           But why does man
Regard religiously this tract
Cadaverous and under band
Of blastment? Nay, recall the fact
That in the pagan era old
When bolts, deemed Jove's, tore up the mound,
Great stones the simple peasant rolled
And built a wall about the gap
Deemed hallowed by the thunder-clap.
So here: men here adore this ground
Which doom hath smitten. 'Tis a land
Direful yet holy—blest tho' banned.[24]

Melville's allusions, pagan and Judeo-Christian, can be dizzying—it is in fact the "method of multitudinous detail,"[25] all too
frequently clashing with the poet's sensory imagination ("Dead,
livid, honey-combed, dumb, fell"), that makes reading *Clarel* particularly arduous. But the poet's overriding mood, his profound
skepticism, will ultimately pierce the poem's afflatus and turn
Clarel into a *katabasis* of psychic exhaustion, an entropic descent
in which Clarel and his fellow pilgrims are left to wander like ship-
wrecked mates the shores of the petrified Dead Sea, itself a symbol
of the receding wave, the geological drying up of faith.

    Clarel is, then, a *katabasis* gone awry, a journey in which the
descent but not the ascent beckons. Some twenty years earlier,
shortly before the publication of *Mardi*, Melville had written to
Evert Duyckinck, "I love all men who *dive* . . . I'm not talking
of Mr. Emerson now—but of the whole corps of thought-divers,
that have been diving & coming up again with blood-shot eyes

since the world began."[26] In the descent of Odysseus in book 11 of the *Odyssey*, in the Homeric *Hymn to Demeter*, in Orpheus's descent into Hades, in Virgil and in Dante, even in Christ's harrowing of hell, we witness the destabilizing of the self, its recoil, and ultimately, its re-ascent. "Poetry, like art," wrote Paul Celan, "moves with the oblivious self into the uncanny and strange to free itself."[27] The Deep is not necessarily a place of horror or extinction but rather one of fragmentation and reintegration, of touching bottom (as Alice does in Wonderland) in order to recoup one's energies and reconfigure the self.

"The Canto of Ulysses" in Primo Levi's *Survival in Auschwitz* is an extreme example of a modern *katabasis*. The author, speaking from the real-life inferno of the camps, valiantly tries to reconstruct in his memory Dante's canto 26, for his sake and that of his young French comrade Jean, otherwise known as Pikolo. Significantly, the chapter begins belowground: "There were six of us, scraping and cleaning the inside of an underground petrol tank; the daylight only reached us through a small manhole. It was a luxury job because no one supervised us; but it was cold and damp. The powder of the rust burnt under our eyelids and coated our throats and mouths with a taste almost like blood."[28] Levi and his Kommando inmates have been literally thrust into a lower circle of the *Inferno*, and Pikolo, descending a rope ladder, will become, for the brief space of an hour, the narrator's deliverer, as re-ascending into "the brightness of the day" they slowly walk together to fetch a pot of soup from the kitchen. Pikolo would like to learn Italian, and Levi immediately—after all, "the important thing is not to lose time, not to waste the hour"—sets out to teach his friend the canto of Ulysses.[29] What may seem an absurd task is revealed as necessary, even obligatory, for patching together half-remembered lines of Ulysses' final voyage becomes a way of recovering and safeguarding Primo Levi's own humanity:

Here, listen Pikolo, open your ears and your mind, you have to understand, for my sake:

Think of your breed; for brutish ignorance
Your mettle was not made; you were made men,
To follow after knowledge and excellence.

As if I also was hearing it for the first time: like the blast of a trumpet, like the voice of God. For a moment I forget who I am and where I am.[30]

In pressing his words (which recall the opening of Inanna's journey) on Pikolo, Levi hears—as if "for the first time" the imprint of Dante's voice, whose own verses reprise Homer. And yet Ulysses' journey on the open sea is repeatedly juxtaposed with Levi and Pikolo's plodding, circular mission to the soup kitchen in the Inferno into which they have been thrust. Their "ascent" from their own *bolgia* is after all only the briefest of respites, and the gaps and holes in Levi's memory are the psychic equivalent of the yawning chasm that awaits them at every turn. To reconstruct Dante's words and their full connotative value ("and I try, but in vain, to explain how many things this 'keen' means"[31]) is to stave off the demon lurking everywhere in the camp. This is driven home with searing irony in the concluding lines of the chapter. Coming to the end of their trek, Levi recalls in a flash the last lines of canto 26:

It is late, it is late, we have reached the kitchen, I must finish:

'And three times round she went in roaring smother
With all the waters; at the fourth the poop
Rose, and the prow went down, as pleased Another.'[32]

Ulysses' ship has gone under, even as moments before he and his crew rejoiced at the sight of landfall. Levi holds back from us the very last line of the canto as he tries in vain to keep Pikolo back from the soup queue. There is still so much to say, to explain to his young friend. But they too are fated to join the "ragged crowd of soup carriers from other Kommandos." Dragging themselves into the queue, amid a babble of tongues, the last line of Dante's Ulysses canto seems to rise from and fall back into the primeval Great Below:

'And over our heads the hollow seas closed up.'[33]

*   *   *

The *katabasis* is, then, a journey into the night of the soul, as in Eliot's reprise of St. John of the Cross, "I said to my soul, be still, and let the dark come upon you / which shall be the darkness of God."[34] It anticipates the second topography and its concomitant genre: the voyage out, and, depending on the narrator's fortune, the homecoming: *nostos*. The examples are myriad: the biblical Exodus, Homer, the voyage of the Argos in Pindar's Pythian 4 and then again in Apollonius of Rhodes, the Anglo-Saxon "The Wanderer" and "The Seafarer," *Sir Gawain and the Green Knight*, *The Rime of the Ancient Mariner*, Browning's "Childe Roland to the Dark Tower Came," "Le Bateau Ivre," Joyce's *Ulysses*. In the twentieth century, Cavafy's "Ithaca" and Mallarmé's *Un Coup de Dés* inaugurated a score of modern and contemporary poems that both set out and put into question the mythopoetic dimensions of the journey poem.

Less known in the West, however, is the pre-Islamic *qasida*, or quest ode. The form originated in the heart of Arabia and has a tripartite structure: the *nasib*, or erotic prelude; the *rahil*, or chase; and the *fakhr*, or boast. The journey's purposeful forward propulsion would have reflected the seasonal migrations of the Bedouin in search of pasture. Each of these sections is further distinguished by obligatory motifs: the deserted campsite, the recalled departure of the beloved bobbing away in her decorated *howdah* (a covered litter), the slaughter of the *naqa*, or she-camel. Thus Imru al-Qays, the earliest of the qasidists, who is believed to have died around 550 CE and whom Muhammad is alleged to have proclaimed the most accomplished of the poets and "their leader to Hell-fire,"[35] launches his *qasida* with the following words:

Rein in your mares and weep, for a love and a campsite
    at the dune's twisted edge between al-Dakhul and Haumal,
Toodih and al-Mikrat, whose traces haven't yet been swept away,
    by the weavings of the southern and northerly winds,
and look at the doe droppings scattered like peppercorns
    in the sandhollows and beds of gravel.
                                            The morning
they bundled their belongings by the thorny acacia and left
    I felt as if I'd sunk my teeth into a gourd.
Holding their riding-beasts back, my companions said,
    "Come, be patient, don't wallow in grief,"
while tears were my only solace, for is there anything
    to lean on in this trackless halting-place?
Wasn't it the same before her? First came Umm al-Hawarith,
    and then her neighbor al-Rabab, from Ma'sal.
Musk drifted from their bodies like the breath
    of the east wind, pungent with cloves.
More tears of longing welled up and started to trickle
    down and streak the strap of my sword.[36]

The *qasida*, and particularly the seven odes or *mu'allaqa* that hung, as legend has it, over the holy Ka'bah, inscribed in letters of gold on the finest Egyptian cloth as prize trophies during the springtime Sacred Months, have remained the pride of the Arab world. Mention al-Qays—or for that matter Tarafa, or Labid, or Antara—and your Arab interlocutor is likely to break into song, whether it be (as in my experience) a merchant in Jerusalem's Old City, a Bedouin in Wadi Rumm in south Jordan, or the teenage daughter of my friend Fathi in the Galilee. In the last case, Mithal didn't actually sing, but rather responded by asking me shyly if I knew of al-Qays's love for Unayza. I thought at first that I had misheard, because the description of his amorous exploits is rather unorthodox and is one of the many reasons Muhammad set himself apart from the likes of al-Qays and his fellow poets. The scene appears in the erotic prelude:

>   Or what
>   of the time I stole into the *howdah*
> hiding Unayza, and she cried, "You bastard, let me out,
>   I'll follow on foot," and when the litter tilted
> she cried even louder, "You're crippling my camel!"
>   And I cried back, "Go on, slacken the reins,
> and don't think you can keep me from plucking your fruit!"
>   I've sneaked at night into many a tent
> of women with child, and mothers sucking their infants,
>   and even steered their hearts from their darlings
> covered in amulets. And when the babe started to bawl
>   she'd twist half of her body his way, and leave
> the other half for me. But another time she fled
>   down the dune and swore we were done.[37]

The poet-hero shoots forward in the second section as he tracks down his prey before circling back to his point of origin in the third, having proved his mettle and his generosity—frequently displaced onto the ritual sacrifice of the she-camel. "He who conciliates not the hearts of men in a variety of transactions, will be bitten by their sharp teeth, and trampled on by their pasterns,"[38] writes Zuhayr, who was also called Abid al-Shir, "the slave of poetry."

Committed to an ethos of tribal survival, the poet, or *sha'ir* ("knower"), celebrated in the *qasida* "the infinite language of the deserts,"[39] which was constantly under threat. The knowledge of the *sha'ir* was manifold. He was tribal spokesman and elegist, arbitrator and lovesick troubadour, warrior and soothsayer. His powers were said to be allied with those of the *jinni*, or desert demon. As such his role was not all that different from the Anglo-Saxon *scop* and the Scots *makar*. All three worked in an oral tradition, and in Old English the alliterative line, with its sharp midline caesura, is strikingly similar to the two hemistiches forming the *qasida*'s basic metrical unit. Measured speech bound the individual to the community, but in the patterning of its voice and its ceaseless movement, it also set the nomad free. It is, in the words of the great Syrian-born contemporary poet Adonis (also known as Ali Ahmed Said), "the search for the self, and the return of the self, but by means of a perpetual exodus away from the self."[40] Here is the last movement of Imru al-Qays's *qasida*, the tribal boast, which in this case turns into a magnificent, panoramic description of torrential desert rains that in their gathering force bespeak an *élan vital*, an inexorable, all-enveloping force of nature that unifies the material world and its heavenly counterpart:

My friend, can you see the faint bolt of lightning?
Look how it flashes in the distance like a flicker
of hands in the thunderhead crowning the skies.
It flares with the brilliance of lamps whose wicks
a recluse has twisted and dipped in oil.
I sat with my companions between Darij
and al-Udhayb, gazing out into the desert fastness.

We reckoned its downpour had swept over Qatan
on our right, even as it drummed down to the left
over al-Sitar and far off Yadhbul.
Then it unloosed
its load over Kutayfa, and thrashed the thorn trees
to the ground, as sheets of rain spreading over al-Qanan
drove the white-hoofed ibex from every nook and ledge.
Not a single palm was left standing in Tayma,
nor any building, save a stone fort;
and when the rains gathered force, Thabir
resembled an old chief bundled in a striped cloak,
while the early morning peaks of al-Mujaymir,
scored with debris, looked like the whirl
of a spindle.
The cloudburst released its waters
over the wastes of al-Ghabit like a Yemeni unloading
his bag of goods for sale, and at daybreak the finches
in the broad wadi were giddy with spiced wine,
while beasts of prey at dusk, drowned in the furthest reaches,
lay stiff on their sides like uprooted bulbs of squill.[41]

What modern texts might fit into the overall structure of the *qa-sida*? Two seminal poetic works come to mind: *Un Coup de Dés* and *The Waste Land*. The affinities of the former text with the *qasida* may be more suggestive than formal, in keeping with the poet's own strictures. But when Mallarmé writes (in his autobiographical letter to Verlaine) that the duty of the poet is "l'explication orphique de la terre,"[42] I have the distinct impression that I am listening to one of the poet-magi of Arabia. And cannot the very opening scene of *Un Coup de Dés*, with its dispersion of words on the blank page—"from the depth of a shipwreck"[43]—be read as the equivalent of the *atlal*, or deserted campsite trope? Granted, we are speaking of a wreckage at sea. And yet the qasidists themselves were wont to speak of the desert in oceanic terms, as in Tarafa's prelude:

> The litters of the Maliki camels that morn in the broad
> Watercourse of Wadi Dad were like great schooners
> From Adauli, or the vessels of Ibn-I Yamin
> Their mariners steer now tack by tack, now straight forward;
> Their prows cleave the streaks of the rippling water
> Just as a boy playing will scoop the sand into parcels.[44]

"Sands immense," Melville writes in *Clarel*, "impart the oceanic sense."[45] Mallarmé's poet-hero Le Maître, whom we encounter early on in *Un Coup de Dés*, is the master-mariner, the helmsman *hors d'anciens calculs* ("beyond ancient reckonings") who must face the yawning deep, the Mallarméan void, a place of despair and defiance, twin emotions never far from the pre-Islamic poet's own daily, far more prosaic encounter in the heart of Arabia—otherwise known as the Empty Quarter—with "the indelible idea of pure Nothingness."[46] So too Mallarmé's evocation of Septentrion, the seven stars of the Big Dipper; his fixing the constellation into place on the folio page in the final movement of *Un Coup de Dés* (the poet's *fakhr*) finds its parallel in Imru al-Qays: "I said, 'sluggish night, give way to morning, though surely / daybreak is no better than you! What a night / you are, with your legion of stars roped to Yadhbul's / summit and the Pleiades fixed in place / by flax twined to solid rock.'"[47]

Even more remarkably (since one can assume Eliot had no more than a passing familiarity with pre-Islamic poetry), *The Waste Land* moves from its own erotic prelude (and multiple remembrances) in the first two sections, "The Burial of the Dead" and "A Game of Chess," to loosely equivalent scenes of the chase or hunt in "The Fire Sermon" (with Tiresias in the role of the desert poet-seer), and ends with a final boast in "What the Thunder Said," in which lightning and "the limp leaves" that "waited for rain, while the black clouds / gathered far distant, over Himavant,"[48] recall al-Qays's own thunderous ending.

These are mythic themes that cut across cultures and civilizations—"icons of structure," to quote Jaroslav Stetkevych, who has also spoken of the *qasida* as encapsulating the sonata form—halt: recall: movement (*allegro*): reprise.[49] Which brings us to the radical rescoring of the *qasida* by American-born Israeli poet Harold Schimmel, who established a reputation as one of the country's most exciting and innovative poets soon after settling in Jerusalem in the early sixties. Here is the ending of the third canto, in my translation, from Schimmel's collection *AR'A* (Earth), published in 1979. The excerpt incorporates lines from Mallarmé's prose poem "Le Nénuphar Blanc" (The White Water Lily), one of many unlikely conjunctions:

A moving plane
cast
shadow

a plot of grass
with eighteen kinds
of flowers

you Jim
barely endured
the Hellenistic

piebald
I rowed and rowed
with a clear

sweeping
drowsy
motion

the fixed
gleam
of the initials

on the bared
oars
reminded us

of our corporeal
existence
upon leaving

the bank
cityward
a store

"water beds"[50]

Schimmel has always been fascinated by foreign literary models
as well as the local epic, "mixing contemporary event," he would
write, "with regional history, first person with persona, narrative
with simultaneous description and harangue";[51] since the nineties
this has extended to the *qasida*, which lends itself to all the above.
There first appeared a series of short, aphoristic reflections on the
qasida form, translated and published in English as *Qasida*:

1. The apparatus of poetry itself, which is today *a poem* as a formal
mode without center, *a qasida*. A concept of form for the complex
poem, *the style of the qasida*, polyphonic, shifting, fickle.

6. A *desert* as a model of a world made concrete in erasure. "In-the-footsteps-of and falling behind." Erasure enforcing a trace of a kind. What was once, is no longer. Mere chicanery. But the whole purpose of the movement was its after-image, an abiding impression as specter of what once was simple being.

60. Thoroughly absorbed in the living moment of the poet-hero's evanescence. And thus engaged in reading traces of himself.

Like a cat twisting back at the defecation content of a hole it just dug.

79. *Rahil* (pedlar: *rahel*, traveling from place to place, linked perhaps to "foot" or "leg": *regel*). Departure on the back of a familiar animal in its role in the chase, desire.

A moving semblance of desire-in-motion from the point of view of ground zero, that's where I am.

105. Qasida. The entire range of speech's art, from the reflective to the emphatic.

127. The complex women of the *nasib*. They have the same connection with reality that a bouquet of flowers has with real flowers in a real field. Nowhere else will you find them with the same density, proximity, combination, disposition in the world of action they represent.

258. Desire is what the poet-hero-subject embodies. Always forward-urging, toward the nearby stopping places. But image and metaphor provide a redundance of braided ties and conjunction. Lines of divergence, loops in the net, criss-cross each and every site.[52]

Then came Schimmel's own *qasida*s, wild and free, "forward-urging" as their Arabian counterparts, yet manifestly triangulated and rethought in the idiom and currency of the present. In the first of six *qasida*s opening Schimmel's Hebrew collection of 2009 *Qasida*, the scene shifts from the traditional abandoned desert abode to a beachside makeshift tent. Here is the modern-day equivalent of the *atlal*, or ruined campsite scene of the beloved, which introduces the erotic prelude:

Is that stick still
           there in the sand
     at its loony angle
             on which once hung

a piece of cloth
       from a dress
    your average rag
        the color of corn

but faded the shade
       of harvest hay
   spun cotton
       a sign of your camp

the site of your
        threesome
  you you
      and the same few-hours' dog

that didn't know
        of barking's power
    orange like a lion
        entirely a creature

of hugs   and often
        mouth to muzzle
   with barely sufficient
        drinking water[53]

Schimmel's stick in the sand and cloth may allude to the opening of the great *mu 'allaqa* of Antara Ibn Shaddad, the poet-warrior would become the subject of the popular Arabic *Romance of Antar*: "Have the poets left a single spot for a patch to be sewn?" while Antara's camel ("huge-bodied as a castle")[54] becomes Schimmel's overfriendly mutt, and the telltale scorched traces of campsite life are reenvisioned as three butts ("to be precise // the filters") and an empty pack of Marlboro Lights: "with several strands of dark / tobacco inside / (American blend) / and at each stub's end / a nicotine stain."[55]

The poet's head-on engagement with the minutiae of the everyday, his visual acuity and delight in tracking the manifold object-world in motion ("like the birth of film / frame after frame / after frame"),[56] finds its parallel in the stasis (halting, looking, remembering) and motion (breaking away, chase, naming-by-way-of-analogy) of the classical *qasida*. Schimmel's prose reflections on the *qasida* make it abundantly clear that he has grasped intuitively the pre-Islamic ode's underlying modernity: its method of luminous detail, its rapidly shifting scenes and moods—a feature that nineteenth-century orientalists would find particularly disturbing—and its unabashed erotics ("And when the babe started to bawl / she'd twist half of her body his way, and leave / the other half for me"); indeed its "narrative with simultaneous description and harangue" anticipates the voice, mood, and technique of the modern lyric. Schimmel's *qasida*s are his own homecoming, his own *nostos*, a circling back to The Land, earthbound Ar'a, in Aramaic, but also HaMakom, The Place (as in Genesis 28:17: "How awesome is this place! This is none other than the abode of God, and that is the gateway to heaven"). Contraries meet head-on, or, as one of Schimmel's personas in *AR'A* puts it:

Symkin himself used
To write on the wall: "God's a wiz"

even the crows on the roof

caw

    "What different things

  link up?" and—

"How

    shall we be hereafter?"[57]

Thirty years later, in Schimmel's Hebrew *qasida*s and his prose tract, the poet extends his poetic journey, his *rahil*, and moves from Greek to Arabic lore, grounding himself further in The Land and its assortment of cultures. "The homage to the original is essential," he would write on Zukofsky's translations of the Yiddish poet Yehoash, "not transference from language to language but regeneration as the materials move from man to man."[58] A boast or *fakhr* is simply one man's reckoning, which in Schimmel's case is laced with self-irony, and rather than self-aggrandizement ends in humility:

That's your dwelling

        for a day

  we take

    an interest in things

  until we recognize

      what they are

    and then we drop them

          if we'd been Adam

we wouldn't have

    named a thing

  let us be

    in our rags of skin

  the end is beyond me

      all that remains

```
          meager footprints
                of you and you


and a dog
        who took you in
     for whatever
              reason


     sorry for
          what's lost
          on our pity
               have pity⁵⁹
```

*   *   *

And so one arrives at the sinuous, questing meander of the arabesque. It is the most visual of the topologies presented here, its origins lying perhaps in the twist and turns of the Jordan River as it carves its bed along the length of the Syrian-African Rift and spills into the Dead Sea. Its human replication can be seen not far from the Jordan on the stucco walls and vaults of the ruined winter palace of the Umayyad prince, Walid Ibn Yazid, or, closer to the source of the Jordan, in the arch at the entrance to the Roman Baths at Hammat Gader. As a literary paradigm it is the playful, self-interrogating, self-proliferating, circular narrative, curving back on itself, and ever deferred. Its Ur-text is *A Thousand and One Nights*, though a lesser known text to the West, the ninth-century polymath al-Jahiz's *Kitab al-Bukhala* (The Book of Misers), would be equally important in its digressions, reported dialogues, and dubious transmission of anecdotal events.⁶⁰ But one might also read *Tristram Shandy* with the arabesque in mind, and closer to our own times, *À la recherche du temps perdu*, in addition to Nabokov, Borges, and Calvino and a score of contemporary novelists. Baudelaire speaks of the arabesque in the *Intimate Journals* as "the most spiritualistic of designs." Might he have seen its constant deferral of meaning as a form of humility wedded to the idea of the infinite, the denial of closure? Mallarmé too will evoke the arabesque and its "dizzying leaps" in speaking of the infinite: "It strikes me that whosoever unleashes the Infinite is under an obligation to make a habit of surprising us, marking that arabesque, the rhythm of which, among the keys of the verbal keyboard, yields itself (as if interrogated by clever fingering) to the use of apt, everyday words."[61] The meander lends itself as well to the essay form—think, for example, of the winding byways of Montaigne's reflections—and is the perfect model for Coleridge's "argumentation in circulo" of the imagination.

Significantly, the arabesque—and this is especially true when speaking of its literary counterpart—covers its own tracks. Hence its resemblance to the skin-shedding serpent: "O patterned psychopomp, / all spiral tail and curlicue of gait /," writes Eric Ormsby, whose collection *Araby* is singularly embedded in the Fertile Crescent. "All accent-lashed, all circumspect of hip, / teach me hollow inside hollow / where the magnet mind can't follow!"[62] In the arabesque's classic form, authorship is constantly challenged: apocryphal texts, misattribution, self-plagiarism, pastiche, are common practice. Authors were not so much accused of as lauded for flaunting their skills as imitators, falsifiers, plagiarists, and forgers. Antara's query "Have the poets left a single spot for a patch to be sewn?" was in effect the cry of a poem's coming into being not as an "original" text but as a successful imitation of an imitation, ad infinitum. Imitation proved to be an intricate affair of recalibration. "Every poem has a memory," writes Abdelfattah Kilito, "and the poet must twist and veil the memory so that his auditors can detect only vaguely the thousand and one poems that lie behind the one they hear. . . . Poetry is the scene of successive incarnations and subtle reincarnations."[63]

Such a novel approach to literature and the arts would have had to have taken place during the early Muslim dynasties, with the shifting of power and prestige from Mecca to Damascus, Baghdad, Isfahan, and later, Cairo and, at the western end of the empire, Cordova and Granada. The influence of the desert receded—or rather, boundaries were nostalgically redrawn and its interior transformed, so that the locus of the deserted campsite became an overriding allegory of lost origins—while new urban centers on the wastelands' margins gained ascendancy. The desert became a forsaken terrain to be traversed by merchants in their long, plodding caravans; over time, I would suggest, these ceaseless crossings and crisscrossings formed vast topographic arabesques: compound, interlocking tracings and retracings of man and beast of burden ("When my camel pads nick the hard flint ground," writes Shanfara, arch-brigand poet of the pre-Islamic era in his *Lamiyyat al-Arab* ["Arabian Ode in 'L'"], "it sends off sparks and chips")[64] which would find their corollary in the calligrapher's art and in the ornamented walls of winter palaces and mosques.

Tracing a poem's pedigree may have originated in the need of scholars, jurists, and grammarians to authenticate the hadith, or sayings about the life of the Prophet Muhammad—and to challenge the propensity to set up false trails. The latter were no doubt largely a product of the uneasy coexistence of multiple schools and heterodoxies, each with its own charges of counterfeit and contested attestations of truth. By the eighth century, when the paper mill was introduced to this part of the world, we are decidedly in an age in which the *rawi* (reciter/transmitter) of a received oral tradition was rapidly turning into a professional copyist, compiler, or anthologist. Even the aforementioned seven golden *qasida*s would have had to be written down at some point, as indeed they were, by Ibn Hammad al-Rawiyya—famous for his prodigious memory and for his forgeries—in the latter half of the eighth century. Are we to believe that these are truly the verses of the great poets of the pre-Islamic era, or might they be the *rawi*'s own embellishments? Arabic poetry and prose thrived on such playful ambiguities of authorship, embracing the digressive indeterminacy of the arabesque as a form of apprehending the world even while asserting (or disguising) one's voice. Borges, speaking like a true latter-day *rawi* of Joseph-Charles Mardrus, last in a line of troublesome translators of *A Thousand and One Nights*, would rightly, stubbornly insist that "it is his infidelity, his happy and creative infidelity, that must matter to us."[65]

So we come to our own postmodern times. Is not the arabesque very much part of our culture of appearances and surface detail, entrenched in the realm of pastiche and misattributed authorship, of self-effacing, discontinuous texts and shifting personal pronouns, of deferral of meaning and nonlinear narrative? Why, for example, would John Ashbery title a poem "Scheherazade" if not to emphasize the ceaseless, wily disposability of narrative? "An inexhaustible wardrobe has been placed at the disposal / of each new occurrence."[66] The poem, like the character of Schcherazade herself, who must cut short her tale at dawn in order to keep the king suspenseful, desirous, in a state of receptivity, operates under the aegis of the suspended sentence—"It was all invitation"[67]—a ploy that would become the trademark of so many New York school poems.

And finally, back to O'Hara. Are not his dodging tactics a form of the arabesque? Even the bravura of *Personism: A Manifesto* sounds not unlike one of al-Jahiz's humorously dubious anecdotes: "That's part of Personism. It was founded by me after lunch with LeRoi Jones on August 27, 1959, a day in which I was in love with someone (not Roi, by the way, a blond). I went back to work and wrote a poem for this person. While I was writing it I was realizing that if I wanted to I could use the telephone instead of writing the poem, and so Personism was born."[68] And just as Schimmel refashions the *qasida*, so O'Hara will revitalize the arabesque: the title "In Memory of My Feelings" announces, with the poet's typical blending of the serious and the parodic, the distance established between the observing (elegizing) and the feeling self:

My quietness has a man in it, he is transparent
and carries me quietly, like a gondola, through the streets.
He has several likenesses, like stars and years. Like numerals.

My quietness has a number of naked selves,
so many pistols I have borrowed to protect myselves
from creatures who too readily recognize my weapons
and have murder in their heart!
                                   Though in winter
they are warm as roses, in the desert
taste of chilled anisette.[69]

O'Hara's motility, his immersion in analogical patterns of thought, in which comparisons proliferate and the self is not so much divided (as in the standard crisis poem) as repeatedly reinvented, call to mind the explosion of correspondences in Arabic and Persian court poetry: stylistic embellishments, figuration, hyperbole ("At times, withdrawn / I rise into the cool skies / and gaze on at the imponderable world"[70]), the art of "semantic overflows,"[71] in Michael Sells's apt description of the Arabic poetic tradition, are the bread and butter of "In Memory of My Feelings." Likewise in O'Hara's evocation of the desert, of his "transparent selves" as serpents "writhing and hissing / without panic," of "Arabian ideas" and numerology, and, in the third section:

The most arid stretch is often richest,
the hand lifting towards a fig tree from hunger
                                   digging
and there is water, clear, supple, or there
deep in the sand where death sleeps, a murmurous bubbling

proclaims the blackness that will ease and burn.
You preferred the Arabs? but they didn't stay to count
their inventions, racing into sands, converting themselves into
so many,
   embracing, at Ramadan, the tenderest effigies of
themselves with penises shorn by the hundreds, like a camel
ravishing a goat.[72]

This would suggest the poet is consciously following at least one narrative thread that might be loosely called mock "Arabic" or "Muslim," or even in its irreverence embracing the sort of ludic powers which would have brought a smile to the face of the pre-Islamic hellfire poet Imru al-Qays.

O'Hara's sloughing of selves—Arab, Persian, Greek, French, Hittite, African, Chinese—takes us back to the first topology, and although there is no apparent descent into the underworld, we do read of "Terror in earth, dried mushrooms, pink feathers, tickets, / a flaking moon drifting across the muddied teeth, / the imperceptible moan of covered breathing, // love of the serpent! / I am underneath its leaves as the hunter crackles and pants / and bursts."[73] It is a phantasmagoria that certainly has the feel of a *katabasis*, a destabilizing of the self or selves, leading "into the uncanny and strange to free itself."

"In Memory of My Feelings" may very well incorporate all three topologies. The cityscape—whether Venice, New York, or Chicago—has now superimposed itself on the topology of the desert, though less as a wasteland than as a place of multiple occurrences. It is at once enchanting, aleatory, and anonymous (the shipwreck of the singular, if I may evoke another poet of the city).[74] Its streets are a continual meander, its architecture a compilation of patterns and vectors and recesses suggestive of our own psychic retreats: "And now the coolness of a mind / like a shuttered suite in the Grand Hotel / where mail arrives for my incognito."[75] Is it not possible to detect, as Schimmel would say, "Motives, evidence, clues, tracks, signs, details?"[76] And is the poem not permeated with a sense of imminent danger? "The dead hunting / and the alive, ahunted."[77] The journey out, intimations of invasions, of battle scenes, victories and defeats, "How many selves are there in a war hero asleep in names? under / a blanket of platoon and fleet, orderly."[78]

Sections 3 and 4 of the poem might be read as a belated erotic prelude, evoking memories of the beloved: "His mistress will follow him across the desert / like a goat" and "I'm looking for my Shanghai Lil."[79] In the fifth and final section O'Hara delivers his boast (the life-affirming *fakhr*), having assumed unabashedly the guise of the serpent (appropriated rather than feared), speaking from within the sinuous folds of the arabesque, "to bend the ear of the outer world," having come full circle, riding on the crest of the poem's driving force, the bounty, the munificence, of its own gifts ("since to move is to love")[80]:

> When you turn your head
> can you feel your heels, undulating? That's what it is
> to be a serpent. I haven't told you of the most beautiful things
> in my lives, and watching the ripple of their loss disappear
> along the shore, underneath ferns.[81]

A fertile crescent for the wanderings of the itinerant poet. Retracing the meanderings of a river, but also the coils of the apotropaic serpent—the charmer's plaything, "naked host to my many selves"[82]—denizen of a rough, dry terrain plunging down, shooting out, or twisting back on itself on the occasion of the poem's transformations. The ground of poetic speech.

Hezekiah's Tunnel

Pitching his tent between the newly constructed Russian Compound and Jaffa Gate, the peripatetic, good-humored English zoologist Henry Baker Tristram could still count on one hand the number of new structures built on the otherwise barren hills surrounding Suleiman the Magnificent's crenellated ramparts. There was British Consul Finn's summer house in Talbia; Schneller's orphanage near the Arab village of Lifta; Montefiore's windmill; Bishop Gobat's Protestant school on Mount Zion. Otherwise the eye roaming from west to east first paused in the shade of Sheikh Muhammad al-Khalili's two-story *qal'a*, or fortress, with its buttresses and high windows, surrounded by olive groves and fig trees—whose leaves resemble giant surgical gloves—before resting on a rippling sea of white tombstones and on the small, impoverished Arab village of Silwan, hugging the rocky slopes of Olivet.

Some years later, in the aftermath of the cholera epidemic of 1866, there was such a pitch of activity outside the old city walls that you'd have thought the Ottoman authorities had lost their keys to Jaffa and Damascus Gates, customarily closed at sundown.

The rocky terrain was rapidly parceled out between the town's various foreign communities: Protestant—the English, German, and American contingents; French Catholic; Russian and Greek

Orthodox; Armenian; and Jewish. The Jews were busy building their first residential neighborhoods, each with its strongman—Montefiore, Rivlin, Rabbi David Ben Shimon—and its mandatory Book of Regulations, whose "fraternal covenant" was concerned with the safety of the residents ("The gatekeeper shall not open the gates to anyone, except by permission of the community's officers or by a letter of permission to be presented to the gatekeeper"); hygiene ("Each and every resident shall instruct those who do his bidding to clean his home daily of all refuse and of every unclean thing, as well as to spray the floors of his home with clean water at least once daily"); and worship ("Every day, following the study of a chapter of the Mishnah, someone shall recite *kaddish derabbanan* for the soul of the departed Judah Tourno, may he rest in peace").[1]

Wed.! Evening. I saw (vaguely): . . . a young man in a Russian hat . . . frantically gesturing up and down with his arm: orders must be followed.

2

Emek Repha'im. The Valley of Giants—huge, dangling presences who slip in and out of the Pentateuch like prehistoric golems. The last Titan was supposedly Og, King of Bashan, who'd stretch himself out nightly on a fourteen-foot-long iron bed. As for the Valley of the Giants, it was—is—a fertile plain coveted by the Philistines and the Israelites just southwest of Jerusalem. Corn must have grown here in abundance, as Isaiah's imagery of a man "[gleaning] the ears of grain in the Valley of Repha'im"[2] suggests.

Repha'im has, moreover, a second and no less important meaning: it is the word for "ghosts," or, to be more precise, for the shades inhabiting the underworld of Sheol, and it appears as such in the later Wisdom Literature. "The Repha'im writhe," Job spits back at Bildad, "in the underworld";[3] and Psalm 88: "Shall the Repha'im arise and praise thee?"

I thought: the voice of the people is the voice of God.

3

The lion sleeps on his paws, content. There are others scattered about the city, but their stance is inevitably vigilant; they growl savagely or sit up erect and proud, like the stone pair in front of the old British Mandate police station near the *sūq* (market). As far as I can tell, this lion, perched above the entrance to 9 Emek Repha'im Street, is the only one to have chosen to bed down in a permanent state of benign resignation. It did not budge when some two years ago the proprietor of the house collapsed on the doorstep from a massive coronary arrest and died, directly under its nose.

I happened to be passing by at the time and noticed the ambulance parked on the sidewalk. I peered into the small, slovenly garden leading up to the entrance and saw three paramedics leaning over an elderly man whose shirt had been ripped open and whose pants were down around his ankles. A woman standing under the portico supporting the gray-speckled Lion of Judah waved one hand in the air as if she were brushing off a fly. She then raised her voice and blurted out, *Lech*, Go, and I realized rather shamefacedly that I was the nuisance her hand was vainly endeavoring to shoo away.

This would be my only encounter with the inhabitants of 9 Emek Repha'im. The house—one of the first in Jerusalem's German Colony—with its blistering wood shutters drawn shut, had always seemed not so much uninviting as blithely disengaged from the increasing bustle of its surroundings.

What was it, then, that had drawn me to the sidewalk—the old man's death, or his sudden, cameo appearance? He had ever so briefly stepped forth into the world. Sprawled on the flagstone, he now appeared to cast over the house and garden a last-minute vitality that was equal perhaps to the vital signs the young paramedics were deftly gauging his body for. The old double portals remained half open: hadn't I followed perversely the ray of light leading into the narrow entranceway?

I'm reminded of the summer evening our neighbor knocked at our front door and led me by the hand to the steps leading up to his balcony. "You must see," he exclaimed, breathing heavily as we stumbled in the dark, "my plant—it blossoms just one night of the year." And indeed rising resplendently from a clay pot was a flower with a cactus-like stem and long, slender petals quivering in the light breeze. Mr. Riklin, in his midseventies, stocky and slow of speech, stood erect as a sentry in front of his prize flower.

Thurs. morning. I read the "Shema" in the morning and as I said "And it shall be unto you for a fringe, that ye may look upon it, and remember all the commandments of the Lord, and do them"—a loud knock was heard. May God have mercy.

4

The link between Titan and Poltergeist may very well be adduced from the verb stem, *raphah*, which means "to sink or relax." In Isaiah 5:24 it is the *sinking down* of hay in flame; in Judges 19:9 the *decline* of day; and in Nehemiah 6:9 the sinking motion is attributed to the hands, as in "Their hands shall be *weakened* from the work." The list of usages goes on: to withdraw, to abate, to lose heart, to let drop, to abandon or forsake, to let alone. The Repha'im-as-Giants may loom large, but only in the metaphoric sense. They are gigantic precisely because they have withdrawn into the mythic past. Having relaxed their grip on the real world, they've become, as the saying goes, mere shadows of their former selves.

3 knocks—exit at once—leave the light on—close the door, but don't lock it—outside by my shack quickly grab round the neck and squeeze, from behind or in front, until he stops moving.

5

Matthias Frank appeared in 1872 on the dusty plain of Repha'im—Wadi al-Waard, Valley of the Roses, as it was then called by the Arabs—with its one conspicuous structure, Qasr el-Ghazal, the Gazelle Tower, guarding the southern approaches to Jerusalem. In wide-brimmed hat and breeches he measured out the land he had just purchased for the Templer Society, a German Christian sect determined to build a miniature Kingdom of God in Ottoman Palestine.

By April the following year he had laid the foundation stone for a boiler plant and home. Inscribed in Gothic letters on the transom of his home were the words EBEN EZER. Another five years and there were a dozen homes with peaked, red-tiled roofs neatly lining the Strassendorf. All that was left was for a caravan of one hundred camels to appear in the spring of 1878, the tall pendulum clocks and eiderdowns of some forty new members strapped to the beasts' flanks.

The Templers produced their own wine, ground their own flour in Frank's steam mill, and engaged in small crafts—carpentry, metalwork, and building. They planted little vegetable gardens in their yards, just like back home—though here the soil didn't yield so readily to their spades and grub hoes—and they congregated weekly at the Tempelgesellschaftshaus, or community center, to raise their pink-fleshed voices to the Lord.

Their lyceum rapidly drew pupils from Russia and the United States, as well as Germany. On the kaiser's birthday free beer was distributed all round, and each home was festooned with flags of the German Empire.

In contrast to the ragtag communities elsewhere in Jerusalem—forever chewing at each other's ears—the Templers were model citizens. Kaiser Wilhelm visited the city in 1898, personally blessed the colonists, who now totaled 392 souls, and cabled the king of Württemberg, informing him of the well-being and industry of his erstwhile subjects.

If they speak of it in the dining-room I'll act surprised. Don't show any signs of worry at his disappearance. If they search for him, I too will participate. Don't leave for town before the afternoon. Arrange my affairs tomorrow and the following days. In case of an interrogation, answer questions. In such a case say I was in my room all the time. Don't talk even of leaving to go to the WC (even if the neighbor says otherwise). Even if they ask about the light that burned in my room, I'll say I was reading. I won't destroy these notes when I awake at 3. I also won't destroy them later. Don't rest on the way. If they ask me how I got scratched, say I fell against the barbed wire fence near the storehouse.

6

A high limestone wall stands between the Templerfriedhof and the local swimming pool. Passing the cemetery on my way to the stationery store I find the gate open and slip in. The tombstones are daubed in shadows cast by the huge pine and cypress trees. In the far corner I spy the diminished figure of the warden. He gives me a cursory nod, then bends over his broom, gently sweeping back and forth, not unlike a child writing his first sentences in a neat and round hand.

The pool, Olympic size, covers the same amount of ground as the Templerfriedhof. It is, one could say, its facing page: its early morning liquid transparency—before the first swimmer creases its surface—suggesting onion paper dyed blue.

I opened the notebook. And a furtive light appeared as a confirmation (was there also a knock? I don't remember now).

7

The indefatigable young British officer of the Royal Engineers, Captain Charles Warren, was the first European to explore Khirbat al-Mafjar. It is 1873, the same year that Matthias Frank settled his family in the German Colony. Warren set out on one of his many excursions outside Jerusalem, this time riding into the Plain of Jericho. Following the course of an ancient aqueduct running along Wadi en-Nuweima, he eventually struck on a heap of ruins. Gilgal, Warren concluded rather impetuously. Just northeast of Jericho, halfway between the city and the Jordan River, the site to fit the biblical coordinates.

Saturday night: I looked at my notes—and heard: a knock. (A sign to read them over—).

8

Mr. Riklin was in fact the one real link I had with the "old" German Colony. It was he who told me that our part of the house had originally been built to serve as the stables of one Martin Fauser, who ran a bakery and confectionary from his house.

The house on 9 Emek Repha'im, Riklin informed me in his low, gruff voice, had belonged to the Templer architect and engineer Theodor Sandel, who lived there until his death in 1902. The napping Lion of Judah was no more than the commercial emblem for a chain of pharmacies run by the Sandel family. The Loewen Apotheke, it appears, had slumbered above the portals of countless apothecaries scattered throughout the fatherland.

As for Riklin himself, I know only the bare facts. He was born in Russia and had wandered about eastern Europe in his youth, living from hand to mouth. Somehow he got to Palestine, enlisted in the British army, saw service in Europe, and eventually settled on Kibbutz Ramat Rachel, on the outskirts of Jerusalem. It was there, if I'm not mistaken, that he met his wife, a German refugee who had spent the war years as an orphan in England.

To the south of the collective settlement sprawled the city of Bethlehem. To the east, shimmering in the heat, loomed the hills of Moab. On clear days one could barely discern in the distance the Dead Sea.

Riklin and his wife would sit in front of their wood shack at dusk, finally at peace. They might have been part of a landscapist's composition—so many painters, beginning with the pre-Raphaelite Holman Hunt, having trekked to this very spot to admire the panoramic view.

The idyll came to an abrupt end in 1948. Shelled by the Jordanians and the Egyptians, the kibbutz members sought temporary refuge in the German Colony, which was for the taking: the Templers, considered enemy aliens during World War II, had been booted off to Australia by the British.

Once the shelling abated, the kibbutz members dismantled their chicken coops and sheep pens, gathered their belongings, and headed back to their homes overlooking the Judean desert. Riklin, however, chose to stay put. One-third of Martin Fauser's house would suit him just fine.

And a faint knocking sound coming from the table. I laced my shoes and unlocked the door. Heard a loud knock. I went out and saw Opher, Yehuda, and a girlfriend of theirs. Fleeting lights outside ... I thought if I don't do what I've been commanded to do, a snake will strike, etc. And a confirming knock was heard. I waited for a furtive light-signal. Then I heard a clear knock.

9

Gilgal.

1. Circle of Stones. The book of Joshua recounts how the waters of the Jordan rushing downstream are dammed up the moment the priests carrying the Ark of the Covenant dip their feet into the strong current. Joshua then leads the seemingly endless file of Israelites across the river and into the Promised Land. Eager to establish his authority over the rather loose confederation of twelve tribes, Joshua isn't going to let the feat go uncommemorated: twelve slabs of stone, gleaming in the dry riverbed, are hoisted onto the shoulders of twelve tribesmen and carried over to the encampment, where they are set down in a sacred circle.

2. Rolled Away. Having set up camp in the Plain of Jericho, Joshua instructs his people to sharpen their knives, for all the males born during the arduous forty-year journey in the wilderness must be circumcised; their foreskins are piled high on what instantly becomes known as the Hill of Foreskins. While the men, young and old, are recovering, God appears to Joshua and

says: "Today I have rolled away from you the reproaches of the Egyptians."[4]

I decided: I'll go out only at the sound of three successive clear knocks coming from the shelter.

10

Mention of Kibbutz Ramat Rachel inevitably brings to mind for me Hebrew poet Noah Stern, who'd moved there in the early fifties in a last-ditch effort to save himself from his own malaise, which he'd sensed almost immediately after disembarking in Jaffa in 1935:

> The lilac that blooms in secret,
> the lilac that blues somewhere in silence—
> reminded me of illusions on one continent,
> and disappointments on another.
>
> But the pungent smell of oranges
> already comes to please and tease me,
> already comes to shower and smother, witnesses
> of life in this homeland.[5]

Stern had been on the kibbutz for a couple of weeks. He'd hoped to be employed there as a teacher and had applied for full membership. For the time being he worked in the *meshek*, or farm, picking crops, cleaning the chicken coops, tending to the livestock. Stern kept to himself, spending most of his leisure time in his small room in a shack, writing. Though he never quarreled with other members of the kibbutz, people saw him as a loner and claimed his conversations were "strange." Perhaps it was this that led the selection committee to decide against accepting Stern as a permanent member of the kibbutz. In early June 1953, Stern was informed that he would have to leave Ramat Rachel within two or three weeks.

The exact date was set for June 19. That same Friday Stern announced he would leave the following Sunday or Monday. This was fine with the kibbutz secretary. On June 20 at four-thirty in the morning, Stern burst into the room of Sokolski, the kibbutz librarian. Sokolski had just enough time to call out, "What do you want?" before feeling Stern's hands tighten around his throat. He fainted and then regained consciousness, apparently after Stern loosened his grip.

Sokolski was fifty-nine years old, lived alone, and suffered from a weak heart; consequently he had an arrangement with the Golovs in the adjoining room that he would knock twice on the wall in an emergency. He did so now, feebly. Golov came running in, switched on the lights, and found Stern bent over Sokolski, his hands still on the librarian's throat. Sokolski's face had turned blue. He was foaming at the mouth and blood trickled from his nose. Golov grabbed Stern and pulled him away. He felt no resistance on Stern's part and when Golov asked Stern why he'd strangled Sokolski, Stern answered, "I wanted to use the bathroom and he wouldn't let me."

Stern was handed over to the kibbutz night watchman, who in turn handed him over to the police. Golov's wife, a trained nurse, rushed Sokolski to the hospital. Why had Stern attacked Sokolski? The librarian claimed to have barely known him. They had talked briefly on three separate occasions, the subject of their conversations always being the borrowing or returning of books from the library. The last exchange had occurred several days before Stern pounced on him. Sokolski happened to walk past Stern's shack.

Stern called out, "Hey, Sokolski, come to my room, I have something to tell you!" Sokolski walked up to the entrance of the shack and, refusing to enter, said, "What do you want?" Stern asked for a certain book and, knowing that Stern was about to leave the kibbutz, Sokolski referred him to the kibbutz secretary.

Shortly after Stern was led away by the police, the kibbutz secretary and a policeman entered his room. Open on the table, among a mass of books and papers, were two notebooks appearing to contain a journal.

I asked whether I should take matches with me—and a furtive light appeared. And a faint knock too.

I I

The alleged site of Gilgal remained unexplored for some sixty years. Finally, in 1935, the Department of Antiquities of the Mandatory Administration decided to start digging. (The excavations would continue right up to 1948, when Israel gained its independence.) It soon became apparent that the ruins had nothing to do with the biblical Gilgal. Nor were the traces of a building they found those of a Christian church commemorating Gilgal, as Warren had hypothesized. In 1953 R. W. Hamilton and Oleg Grabar, two young archeologists, picked up where the old digs left off, and found themselves reconstructing the remnants of a lavish Arab winter palace and bathhouse dating from the Umayyad period.[6]

Ever since the discovery of Caliph Hisham's name among graffiti on the southwestern corner of the place, the local population, guidebooks, and tourist guides—first Jordanian and then, in the aftermath of the Six-Day War, Israeli—have viewed the caliph, who ruled during the first half of the eighth century, as the rightful builder and owner of Khirbat al-Mafjar.

I thought: "at 3 o'clock"—and a knock was heard (not hard). (A sign to go out?) 11 o'clock. "Soon?" A secret knock from the shelter.

12

Noah Stern's journal entries,[7] or *jottings*, as he called them, would be used by the prosecution to prove that the attempt on Sokolski's life had indeed been premeditated. It seemed equally obvious that the defendant was suffering from some form of mental disorder. Stern, however, refused to be examined by a psychiatrist, claiming all along that in his search for a W C, he had merely stumbled into Sokolski's room, and that it was the librarian who had started the altercation. As for the incriminating notebooks, Stern insisted they were not a personal journal but rather the draft for a story in which two men fight over a woman and one jealously plots his rival's murder. He did, however, admit to hearing on occasion strange knocking sounds in his room. Stern told the court, "I read once in the *Encyclopaedia Britannica* that people sometimes hear knocking sounds in their homes which they have difficulty explaining. The article used the German word *Poltergeists*, that is, spirits, or *geists*, that knock, *poltern.*"

I thought how in fact I'd rehearsed in my mind the entire operation— and light-signals appeared and a restrained knock—confirmations!

13

Perhaps all that's needed is to set out from two fronts at one and the same time, like the hewers of Hezekiah's tunnel in the eighth century BC who bored their way underground from both directions simultaneously. Fearing his water supply would be cut off by the approaching army of the Assyrian Sennacherib, King Hezekiah ordered his engineers to dig a tunnel from the spring of Gihon, in the exposed valley of Kidron, to the Pool of Siloam, which was situated within the walls on the west side of the city. Using hand picks, the two teams of laborers worked from opposite ends of the conduit and followed a circuitous course of some 583 yards. The hewers met "miraculously" somewhere in the middle, their course dictated in all probability by natural fissures in the rock where water trickled through.

This evening the first Saturday night party in the "office" of the teachers' college . . . facing me, from the stone house, rises the songs of the youngsters who gathered for a modest Saturday party. . . .

At 11 o'clock I asked: "Will it be soon?"

The answer—a secret knock from the shelter and as I am writing this a light too.

14

Little is known of Hisham. The tenth caliph of the Umayyad dynasty ruled the Arab world for twenty years. Soon after his death the Damascus-based dynasty collapsed, and the center of power shifted to the Abbasids in Baghdad. An able if rather austere figure—in sharp contrast to his brother, the amorous Yazid II, whom he succeeded when the latter died of grief (so it is said) after one of his singing girls choked on a grape he had playfully flung into her mouth—the caliph maintained a palace and bathhouse, Qasr al Hayr al-Ghabri, near the Euphrates in northern Syria. Hamilton describes the palace as being of "sober taste and economical scale,"[8] something which certainly cannot be said of

Hisham's alleged estate in Jericho, with its vaulted arcades, its reception hall with interlaced roundels of busts staring down from the central cupola, its statues of bare-breasted girls holding bouquets of flowers, and its elaborate system of indoor pools.

11:12 A knock. "Indeed?" A very strong light.

15

"What an unusual trial," Noah Stern's attorney declared after the poet had taken the stand for two consecutive days. Stern needed to talk, and talk he did, beginning with his youth in Lithuania, his precociousness in school, his move at seventeen to Canada and then to Harvard University for four years, his decision to cut short his graduate studies in literature at Columbia University and immigrate to Palestine in 1935, and finally his joining the Jewish Brigade and serving with the British in Europe during World War II.

Stern knew he was there to refute the evidence thrust against him by his own journal entries. And yet his efforts to convince all present in the courtroom that the journals were actually the draft for a crime story were largely unsuccessful. Reading the transcripts of the trial, particularly the long section in which the poet speaks in his own defense, one cannot help feeling that Stern's real motive for taking the stand was to vindicate himself as a writer and poet.

Hence Stern's speech gravitated toward the past. He was forty-one, increasingly taciturn, solitary in his habits, and incapable of holding a job for any length of time—the last blow having come when Ramat Rachel voted not to accept him as either a member or a teacher at their college.

Stern managed to publish his poems, short fiction, essays, and book reviews in the literary supplements of the local Hebrew papers, yet few people realized the extent of his originality.[9] In 1941 he published a long poem, "Stopgap Letter," which may well be Israel's first and, to this day, finest modernist poem. It was ignored, and half a century later it remains largely unread. At his death, several hundred copies of his translation of *The Waste Land*, privately published in 1940, were found stacked on the floor of his one-room apartment.

Was Stern actually wringing the neck of Israel's reading public when he tried to strangle the librarian of Ramat Rachel?

Convicted of attempted murder, Stern spent five years in prison. He was admitted to a psychiatric hospital soon after his release and died by his own hand in 1960. A collection of his poems was finally published in 1966. A second, enlarged edition—long out of print—appeared in 1974.

11:25 A knock (from the shelter). I thought, soon . . .

16

The shutter opens and shuts, slicing off an instant of reality in a single stroke, like the blade of a guillotine.

A photograph of Matthias Frank and his family. Matthias, in overcoat and fur hat and sporting a shovel beard, stands erect in the back row, flanked by his two elder sons. His gaze is fixed to the left of the camera. One of his sons is holding a homburg, and his wife is seated in front of him with his elder daughter; all gaze in the same direction.

The rest of the family stares straight into the box camera. Seated on low stools in the front row are the two young daughters, in ankle-length dresses and matching V-shaped vests. Each has an anchor embroidered on her shirt. The girl at the far end of the photo balances a leather briefcase against her leg while leaning her right arm on the thigh of her older brother, who is sitting behind her. This brother, exceedingly handsome in a gray flannel suit, sits straight-backed as a Prussian horseman. The second young daughter, leaning against her mother's knees, holds a basket of flowers in her right hand. A fifth child, wearing a sailor's hat and undoubtedly the youngest of the sons, stands in front of his father, one hand posed on his mother's shoulder, the other holding a book. His older brother stands behind him, balding and wearing a three-piece suit; he in turn has placed his own hand on the boy's shoulder.

The positioning of the hands intrigues. They soften the bold—if somewhat forlorn—look in the eyes of Matthias and his family, and suggest an intimacy running counter to the rigid vertical axis of the figures.

Underground conditions but no formal underground and the signal of three consecutive clear knocks from the shelter—I asked. (And yesterday I heard repeated such a threefold knock from a different corner of the room.)

17

The year the British began excavating Hisham's palace also happened to be the year Noah Stern arrived in Palestine. "A Woman in Jericho," dated September 1936 and published posthumously, attests to Stern's visit to the ancient biblical site:

Ah, what are you thinking, proud negress,
mocking through thick, sunburnt lips,
upright under the slave-burden,
your steps measured, attentive-drowsy—

what crosses your mind, woman, furtively mocking
what's going on—the faint sign in the sand
the daywake leaves, gathered into the past?
What is the black whisper
of your laughing-hostile-loving eye,
gazing from the mound abutting a grove of palms,
gazing at the desert calm, shutting an eye, lying in wait
for he who comes—familiar yet strange approaching from the
  west
toward a known yet unknown landscape among tents of the east?

Jericho! Your faint aroma filled my nostrils, wafted
it seemed from fragrant fields in distant time, when the heart
stirred and sucked sweetness from dusk-of-a-woman's face—
  Jericho!
Horror of antiquity.[10]

*11:35 A light knock (as always from the shelter) (a knock approxi-
mately every ten minutes). The voice of the people is the voice of God.
"That murderer!" A bright furtive light. Linked with all the destroyers
and betrayers a signal—bright light. The light-signals got brighter
yesterday while I was writing these notes appearing in accordance with
the stations on the path I had previously crossed. Fleeting light.*

18

"A trifling detail,"[11] the modeling of the eyelids of the stucco figures, would function as a decisive clue in confirming Hamilton's
reservations concerning Caliph Hisham's dubious role in the
building and use of al-Mafjar.

The eyelids of the figures found in the palace were rendered
differently from those found in the bathhouse. The former were

stuck on like rings of plaster around the eye; the latter were modeled smoothly from the surface of the eye socket and cheeks.

Hamilton already knew that the palace and bathhouse had been built at different times. Lime crusts in the pipes, and deposits of soot and ash in flues and furnaces proved that the bathhouse had been in use for some time, whereas the palace appeared never to have been completed.

We have, then, two masters: one of the palace who worked in the method of "stuck-on" eyelids, and one of the bathhouse who had undoubtedly perfected his own style some years earlier.

3 consecutive knocks—and he's outside! A double and triple sign. The giant spider—a sign of punishment! If—first of all I must prevent others from being harmed by him.

"Successful times."

12.48 A knock and strong fleeting light (I thought: better I end up in hell than others suffer because of my inaction) a very bright light.

19

As early as 1829, in his preface to *Les Orientales*, Victor Hugo wrote, "Au siécle de Louis XIV on était Helleniste, maintenant on est Orientaliste." Stern cannot escape the allure of the East: like his predecessors—I am thinking in particular of the long list of painters, beginning with Ingres, Jean-Leon Gerome, Delacroix, who seemed bent on painting the Levant through a peephole—the poet transforms the arid landscape into a narrative of thwarted desires.

Though weighted down by a thick impasto of adjectives, "A Woman in Jericho" intrigues: its lurching syntax and compounding of words conveying mimetically the poet's advance and retreat from the dark, Arab woman's gaze; the "black whisper" (the Hebrew *lachash*, meaning both "whisper" and "charm," may have originally stood for serpent-charming) of the "laughing-hostile-loving eye" of the East.

But Stern is also testing out and adjusting his own literary Hebrew to his new surroundings in Hebrew-speaking Palestine. Here, then, are the poet's first efforts to abandon the felicities of a pristine, neo-biblical Hebrew—a melodic, incantational Hebrew embodied in the poetry of Chaim Nachman Bialik, who died a year before Stern's arrival in Palestine—for something more ragged, even prosaic and irregular, like the hard, dusty terrain of the Jordan River valley.

Such a deliberate rough-handling of language was to become Stern's trademark and, in a sense, his "slave-burden" under which, misunderstood and increasingly isolated, he would eventually collapse.

When did the threads begin to unravel? There's certainly something ominous in the figure of the leering, haughty, dark-skinned woman of Jericho, whose allure is tinged with terror, her "attentive-drowsy" gait suggesting the sinuous movements of a courtesan—a Kuckuk Hanem, as evoked in Flaubert's letters from Egypt, or a dancing girl, one of a troupe, emerging from Ibn Walid's domed bathhouse. She is elusive, it would occur to me later, as the haunting song of the local grackles off the steep walks of the dry ravines near Jericho.

She mocks furtively, insinuatingly, she winks, as the Hebrew *remez* (hint) would imply. And seventeen years later the same hopelessly charged word will resurface—repeatedly, insistently—in Stern's journals, as will its contiguous *ot-hadak*, "the faint sign."

12:03 A knock and steps. I went out but didn't see anybody. (15 minutes after the previous knock—in regular intervals.) Maybe I should

go out every 10 minutes—a very strong light, I'll go out whenever I
hear the sound of a knock.

20

THE SILOAM INSCRIPTION 701 B.C.

The boring completed.
This is the story of the boring through.
As workmen lifted their picks,
Each toward his neighbor,
Three cubits left to be cut,
Each heard the voice of the other
Calling his neighbor through a crack in the rock
On the right side.

The day of the boring through
The hewers wielded their pickaxes
Each to meet his fellow,
Pick to pick, and the waters gushed
To the pool in great quantities,
As the stonecutters huddled in delight,
In the belly of the earth.[12]

This man has come to murder me!—a bright furtive light.

21

Buried in the dust at the foot of the bath gate tower, Hamilton and
his colleagues found the head and lower body of a near life-size
figure clad in the royal garments—pearl-edged coat, trousers, and

jeweled belt—of a caliph. There was no question that the caliph, hand on sword, feet firmly planted on a lion pedestal, had looked down with the authority of a sovereign from a large niche at the very top of the tower at all who approached the domed portal.

Could this be Hisham? Inspection of the head revealed a curious fact: the eyelids were stuck on and ring shaped; this would indicate that the figure must have been carved by the palace master, who worked, we know, some years after the master of the bathhouse.

The caliph's bulging eyes led Hamilton to conclude, in effect, that the niche stood empty for a number of years. "A millionaire with a taste for ornamental statuary"—here one must let Hamilton speak for himself—

> building his pleasure palace, will not normally instruct the architect to finish the figures of slaves and entertainers first but leave his own portrait for a later occasion. If he does just that, being also ruler of half the world, we are bound to seek some more than ordinary reason. There is one simple observation: the owner must not be the ruler but his heir. While the caliph lives, no private effigy, certainly no symbol of sovereignty, can be openly displayed. The niche must be left empty. When the owner inherits, the portrait may be seen: it will show the ruler of Islam.[13]

12:25 A knock. I went out and didn't see anybody. From somewhere in the near distance I heard a couple whispering (to be precise: the voice of a girl). 12:30 A car passed . . . the plan is ready to be executed.

22

It must be at least ten years now since I first read Stern's long poem, "Stopgap Letter." I had been browsing in an English bookshop on Salah a-Din Street in East Jerusalem, and found a slim volume of translations of Hebrew poetry wedged between large, hardbound tomes on Middle Eastern affairs with such titles as *The Struggle for Palestine*, *Trial and Error*, *Memoirs of King Abdullah of Transjordan*, and *The Eastern Question*. The volume was edited by the poet Dennis Silk. At the time, I knew him only by sight.

Leaning against a wall of books, I soon found myself engrossed in "Stopgap Letter," in Harold Schimmel's translation. The long line and quirky syntax convinced me I was reading a poet of the "new generation," a native-born Israeli who'd undoubtedly read Whitman, Crane, and maybe even John Ashbery. Here was a poet of the avant-garde, I told myself, someone who spoke to us from the future. I read on—until I came to the last line, "World, you will be done," under which Schimmel had quietly inserted the date, 1942.

The poem, it turns out, was written during the winter of 1941 in Jerusalem, where Stern had recently moved. He had previously lived and worked—sporadically, as a teacher and lecturer—in Tel Aviv. At the age of twenty-nine he had had hopes of making a new start in his "feverish-sad city."[14] Within the year, however, Stern would be off again, now as an enlisted serviceman in the British army.

Years go by like winds on the worlds' shell
Naked homeland   for all of our life.
Just yesterday we spilled out hearts, dipped an eye
From the glimpsed in a window, between opaque curtains,
Listening deeply to the Appassionata, in dulled midnight's incense.
Today we say: the search for the infinite,
Or the finite and absolute, does not lead us
To a dusty patrol in tomes of morocco leather,
To a marathon tour among thoughts of the great who died.
We live in the world! And if no more is given
Than archeo-rubble and left-overs, if the whole terrestrial
    structure

Is a narrow tack of embroidery on the hem of the empty heavens,
If each tense exertion is compared to a kaput spring
And our bodies snared and broke   wherever they wait to leap
    forward—
The notched particulars will make an all-inclusive theater in its
    limits,
And daily life—a stage for symbol divination.[15]

Who comes to kill you . . .

23

Kitab al-Aghani. The Book of Songs. Ibn Khaldun called this vast
compendium of poetry and music, literary anecdote, and social
history, compiled in the tenth century by Abu al-Faraj al-Isfahani,
"The *Diwan* [Register] of the Arabs."

Purchasing the *Kitab al-Aghani*, the redoubtable Buyid vizier
Sahib Ibn Abbad, who'd lug thirty camel-loads of books with him
whenever he set out on a journey, was now willing to crisscross
the desert waste with al-Isfahani's volumes and no other texts.

It was to the pages of al-Aghani that Hamilton turned finally
to unravel the identity of the founder of Khirbat al-Mafjar. For
Hisham's heir was known to be his nephew, the bon vivant Walid
ibn Yazid—aesthete, companion, and patron of singers, "the best
poet and marksman of the Umayyads"—whose poor leadership
(he was, rather predictably, assassinated within a year of assuming
office) is well compensated for by the evocation of his character
and poetry in Isfahani's *Diwan*:

The name you'll hear whispered is Imam Walid
wherever I go, in silks shot with gold.

My passion is music (and stealing into bed
with my latest love). I couldn't care less

who says what, just keep filling my cup
with more of the same. I may be a sot
but I certainly know that paradise
is the last place to look for the dark-eyed Houri.[16]

12:35 The van is returning. I thought: "We (on principle) have decided, and one will carry it out"—a number of bright fleeting lights.

12:37 A faint knock . . . I went out. Didn't see anybody . . . I thought, he has been instructed to appear by my room.

24

The other day, coming home from the grocer's, I passed a group of teenagers standing next to one of the Templer homes on our street. Facing the group was a young woman recounting the street's history. I lingered for a moment and then continued home, catching in the air before leaving one word, *Balak*. Balak? I thought to myself . . . the word seemed vaguely familiar. Once home I recalled that the teacher, opening a book, had commenced reading to her students from its pages. The book, too, now seemed familiar. It then dawned on me that Balak was the name of the dog who wanders somewhat aimlessly up and down the narrow streets of Jerusalem for over one hundred pages in S. Y. Agnon's *Tmol Shilshom* (Only Yesterday). Could Agnon have had Balak visiting our neighborhood in a phantasmagoric parable set in Palestine, circa 1910?

Balak's odyssey begins in the neighborhood of Mea She'arim when he approaches a housepainter. This housepainter—whom the reader knows to be named Yitzhak, the main character in the novel, an immigrant, or *oleh*, who had aspired to live the life of a pioneer and eventually finds himself scrounging for a living among Orthodox Jews—dribbles in paint on the stray's back the words *Mad Dog*. From then on Balak's life is made miserable. He is kicked and beaten and pelted with stones. Hounded out of the neighborhood, he wanders from one lonely hovel to another and in time becomes precisely what the label states him to be: raving mad. At last the stray (for once the suggestiveness of the English word *stray* enhances the Hebrew) returns to Mea She'arim and sets his teeth into the flesh of the housepainter whose prank had turned his life into a nightmare. As he does so Balak imagines that Yitzhak's blood will quench his thirst and bring rain to the parched land.

Leafing through the pages of *Tmol Shilshom* (published in 1945 and perhaps Agnon's grimmest indictment of the schismatic world of Jerusalem), I soon found the passage that the teacher must have read to her class as they stood outside the two-story stone house on the corner of Emek Repha'im and Patterson, a house built by the Templers and now serving as a shelter for wayward girls.

Scavenging for food, Balak wanders into the new neighborhoods of Jerusalem, far from Mea She'arim. He finds temporary refuge in various Christian quarters outside the old city walls, first with the Prussian master of the railway station, then with priests in a monastery. Finally he wanders about Abu Tor and from there—ever sniffing out odors—skirts the margins of the German Colony, lest he be caught, strapped to a harness, and forced to replace the mule treading the grindstone in the local flour mill. The very same mill, I told myself, built by Matthias Frank and operated by his sons at the turn of the century.

The man approached me today after supper, as I left the hall! "Kill"
(Strong light). Coughing sound from outside. "Come in for a minute."
"I'd rather stand outside." 1:30 A light knock. I went out and then
returned.

25

It is recounted in the *Kitab al-Aghani* how one day Walid ibn
Yazid sent for Ma'bad, famed for his singing throughout the
Fertile Crescent. The singer, barely having time to shake off the
dust from his long journey, was ushered into a room with a pool
adjoining the *majlis*, or reception room.

Ma'bad found to his utter surprise that the pool had been filled
with rose water mixed with musk and turmeric, and that an embroidered curtain had been let down between its two ends. Ma'bad
was enjoined to sit cross-legged on a carpet at one end of the pool.
The voice of the chamberlain, or *hajib*, rang out: "Greet the caliph, Ma'bad!" Having done so, he heard a voice answer his greet-
ing from behind the curtain. The same voice then named a song
for Ma'bad to sing. As the last notes of Ma'bad's song faded in
the air the curtain was raised by slave girls, and Walid, the young
and impetuous caliph, stepped out, tore off a scented robe, and
plunged into the pool. As he came out of the pool the slave girls
gave him freshly censed clothes. Walid took a drink from a large
cup, offered the cup to the singer, and named another song for
Ma'bad to sing. This was repeated three times.

Ma'bad was well recompensed, returning to Medina with
17,000 *dīnār*s and the caliph's cautionary words still ringing in his
ears: "Oh, Ma'bad, he who seeks provision from kings, will not
divulge their secrets."

At 10:03 I asked whether to go out (I felt sleepy) and after a couple of seconds I heard a knock. I went out . . . 2:23 A knock . . . just before this I thought: I have nowhere to go.

26

And one night, with a breeze mildly ruffling the branches of the dew-soaked olive trees, Agnon's Balak wags his tail in a sleepy neighborhood and hums to himself these verses:

> Eyes to the ground
> no candle flares
> under starry skies
> not a sound
>
> awake I scamper
> over the earth
> but peace reigns
> in cleft and plain
>
> nobody comes or goes
> across my path
> so why stick up
> my nose
>
> the night's young
> the day's far
> before my lids close
> and seal my eyes
>
> across the land
> nobody comes or goes

the flesh is still
Bow-bow Bow-wow.

3:05 A knock from across the end of the corridor just when I insisted I saw a bright star falling (before that I felt weak in the body and sleepy). (Doubts.)

3:25 A knock. I went out. Silence.

27

Then there was the time that Walid summoned the singer Utarrad to his palace. Again the singer was enjoined to sit at one end of a small pool. This pool, however, was just large enough for a man to turn around in and was lined with lead and filled with wine. The description fits perfectly the small unheated room with two tanklike basins (lined with a local gray stone that resembles lead) directly behind the reception room at al-Mafjar.

Having greeted the caliph, the *al-Aghani* recounts, Utarrad was asked by him to sing a particular tune: "So I sang to him. I had barely finished when, by God, he tore apart an embroidered robe that was on him, worth I know not what, flung it down in two pieces, and plunged naked as his mother bore him into the pool; whence he drank, I swear, until the level was distinctly lowered. Then he was pulled out, laid down dead to the world, and covered up. So I got up and took the robe; and no one, by God, said to me 'take it' or 'leave it.' So I went off to my lodging, amazed to see the liveliness of his mind and the violence of his emotions."[17]

3:30 A quick knock after I said to myself: three knocks—and I do it. I went out too. Also prior to the one knock. If I run into him outside— do it.

28

An essay in "archeo-rubble," I told a friend who had asked what I was up to—though perhaps it would have been more judicious to mention the arabesque, a form that repeatedly denies or negates closure; hence the proliferation of open geometric and vegetal forms at Khirbat al-Mafjar. Walid's dancing girls and wide-eyed helmeted men are trapped in an elaborate pattern of ornamental foliage. Meaning, iconographic significance, the representation, say, of a winged horse or of a fox tearing at a cluster of grapes, suggestively teases our thought, but only for a moment: no sooner has the eye paused on a recognizable figure than it is overwhelmed by an exuberance of arbitrary surface detail. The inexhaustible variation of designs points again and again to the possibility of infinite growth. Whoever stepped into the reception hall of the young Umayyad prince after a long and arduous journey in the desert wastes stepped into a cool interior of pure forms.

Particularly in its early manifestations during the rule of the Umayyads, when the aniconic doctrine hasn't yet come into being, the arabesque resembles the dream: Eros, in the guise of meaning, desire's proxy, must contend with the infinite possibilities of the surface or manifest narrative. Individual personages crowding the theater of our dreams can't help but subordinate their "lives" to the bombardment of surface detail, of "notched particulars."

"It is as though a richly orchestrated symphony had been frozen in space,"[18] writes Oleg Grabar of the ornamentation covering the walls of the winter palaces of the new Umayyad aristocracy, a landed gentry seemingly intent on building their country establishments on the margins of the desert.

In 747 AD an earthquake rumbling through the Jordan River valley razed Walid's palace and bathhouse—a sign, perhaps, or omen, like Stern's three knocks, of the imminent collapse of the Umayyad dynasty.

I said: I've decided—after three knocks, I do it. 3:50 A knock. I went out. Quiet . . . A knock followed immediately by another knock. I stepped out and saw hanging in the sky above the house a giant star— exactly like a small moon, but brighter than the moon! And as I was looking at it there appeared the signal: a shooting star. The matter's clear. Signs and wonders.

29

Two pale-yellow gazelles are nibbling at the young shoots of a pomegranate or apple tree. They appear oblivious to the plight of a third gazelle to the right of the tree trunk, buckling under the weight of a lion that has dug its claws into the gazelle's flanks. The mosaic, with its tapestry-like border, remains intact. The theme of the artwork, which was found in the bathhouse guest room, or *diwan*, is reminiscent of hunting scenes depicted in Persian carpets of the time, and its style recalls the naturalism of Roman murals.

The large, domed guest room was the most extravagantly decorated in the estate. Walid's guests, pausing from their courtly pleasures, must have feasted their eyes on the brilliantly hued mosaic there. Could a message have been gleaned in the midst—at the still center—of the fluid, polymorphic world of the arabesque? Were desert travelers lured into the hall and distracted by a swarm of interlacing forms only as a prelude to their being gently and invisibly nudged forward until their gaze fell upon the tenuous fate of the three gazelles?

To this day it's not uncommon to spot the small, roaming, "desert-loving" Asian antelope (or gazelle) in the Jordan valley region. It may even be seen skirting the fringes of Jerusalem, darting behind lichen-speckled boulders and into a pine grove at the first sound of human footsteps.

The English word *gazelle* is in fact a cognate of the Arabic *ghazal*. It acquired, moreover, a second meaning in Arabic: early on in the history of Arabian poetry, the word *ghazal* stood for the beloved. In the eighth century, during the reign of the Umayyads, its meaning was further elaborated on, so that the word *ghazal* represented a certain kind of refined and urbane love lyric. One of its practitioners, perhaps its last virtuoso during the first phase of its development—for the *ghazal* lyric, revived by the Abbasid poets, would eventually spread to medieval Persia and Turkey—was Walid ibn Yazid.

Walid knew his days to be numbered as soon as his uncle Hisham grudgingly delivered the caliphate into his hands. There can be no question with whom the young libertine identified in the mosaic.

Suffering and supplication can't exist in everybody's eyes falsely! On his side Germans and betrayers. He systematically chased me away and I almost died from lack of food.

30

There was a time one could walk from Jerusalem to Jericho, setting out early in the morning from Mount Scopus, or else taking the shorter route from Wadi Kelt, midway between the two points.

From the monastery of Saint George one had but to follow the ancient watercourse hugging the wall of the gorge, which some three hours later fanned open onto the Plain of Jericho.

It was on one of these hikes that I first saw bands of glossy blue-violet Tristram grackles soaring in swift, tight loops above the rock face. These birds, perched on the ledges, hollows, and mouths of the caves once populated by scores of Byzantine anchorites (Meinardus, author of a pamphlet on the monasteries of the wilderness of Judea, called them *celliots*), look from a distance like blackbirds or starlings.

But pushing off from the rock face, its chestnut-tipped wings stretched out, the local grackle announces its true identity in the abandon of its three-note song: a melancholy "rich and musical roll," as Henry Baker Tristram wrote in 1863 of the bird that would soon bear his name. "The wildest and shyest of the denizens of these desolate gorges," he noted attentively, in the inscaped accents of yesterday's explorer.[19]

There was no knock and I decided to go out without being instructed to do so—(immediately the horse came toward me and then it too approached the window). Then it more or less moved away.

"Who Keened over the Bones of Dead Encampments"

ON THE *HANGING ODES* OF ARABIA

Hammad al-Rawiya, last of the true *rawi*s, or transmitters of tribal poetry, was renowned among the newly urbanized Arabs of Damascus and Baghdad for declaiming poems he had heard recited by the Bedouin of the Arabian heartland. In the latter half of the eighth century he put together a collection of seven remarkable poems known collectively as the *Mu'allaqat*, or *Hanging Odes*. These poems have been shrouded in mystery; and though we have already encountered, briefly, its first practitioner, Imru al-Qays, I would like here to delve deeper into their origins, the properties and dynamics of their form, their desert ethos, and the dubious, "forged"—as Abdelfattah Kilito would have it—biographies of their fabled, magnificent seven.

Long before the rise of Islam, legend tells that the poems were transcribed in letters of gold on the finest Egyptian linen and suspended from the Ka'bah in Mecca as trophies during the Sacred Month of Peace, when the Bedouin laid down their arms and made their annual pilgrimage to the fairgrounds of 'Ukaz, near Mecca. Rival clans mingled in the marketplace, and when not buying and selling their wares and feasting, gathered around as the *rawi*s swayed and pitched their lines to the rapt audience. Could these performances have been transcribed at such an early date? The notion has been contested by both medieval and modern scholars of Arabic poetry. Yet the legend lives on, bolstering the iconic status of the *Mu'allaqat* in the collective imagination of the Arab-speaking world. The image of pagan poetry hung from the holy shrine of the Ka'bah serves to bind the ancient world of desert lore to Islam, and the poets themselves—Imru al-Qays ("The Vagabond Prince") Tarafa ("The One the Gods Loved"), Zuhayr ("The Moralist"), Labid ("The Man with the Crooked Staff"), Antara ("The Black Knight"), Amr Ibn Kulthum ("The Regicide"), and Harith ("The Leper")—have passed into legend, each lapped in a vast oral tradition.

* * *

The *Mu'allaqat* are the most famous—and among the earliest—examples of the *qasida* (commonly translated as "ode"), a poetic form that typically runs to some hundred and twenty lines. The term may derive from the root *qasada*, meaning "to aim" or "go forward," or else from *qasar*, "to break," in reference to the mandatory division of each line into two rhythmically equal halves—a binary thrust and parry not unlike the alliterative line in Anglo-Saxon verse. The *qasida* is distinguished as well by the masterly application of a wide range of quantitative meters and a single, unifying end rhyme announced in the second hemistich of the first line. Earlier, introducing Imru al-Qays, I mentioned its division into three distinct movements: erotic prelude, chase, and boast, each punctuated by a series of obligatory motifs that are modified and reshuffled with great ingenuity.

The first such motif, with which each of the *Mu'allaqat* begins, is the *atlal*, an evocation of the abandoned encampment of the poet's beloved. Traces of her tribe's ephemeral presence—charred firewood, blackened hearthstones, shards of pottery, shreds of wool, camel dung—are found in the black terrain, and these touch off anguished riffs on love and loss. All that is needed is the faintest sign, a token of an ancient passion, and remembrance ignites like a fuse.

Here, then, is Imru al-Qays's *atlal* in two distinct English versions. The first was rendered into English by William Jones in 1782. Jones, in effect, introduced Arabic verse to the English reader, and it is perhaps not unrelated that some twenty years later Wordsworth would incorporate the prophetic, "Semi-Quixote" figure of "an Arab of the Bedouin Tribes" into his own blank-verse *Prelude*:[1]

Stay—Let us weep at the remembrance of our beloved, at the sight of the station where her tent was raised, by the edge of yon bending sands between Dahul and Haumal,

Tudam and Mikra; a station, the marks of which are not wholly effaced, though the south wind and the north have woven the twisted sand.[2]

The second version, by Irish poet Desmond O'Grady, offers a modern take on the same dramatic pulling-to-a-halt opening frame:

Halt here friends.
Allow me private pause alone
to remember a love, a longing, an unrequited right
here where the sand dune's rim whorls between where
we've abandoned and where we're bound for.

Here you'll still see
the old camp markers
despite that dangerous whirl
of the south wind,

nerves' nag of the north wind.
Here where they staked out their haggard,
there in those parched hollows
you can still see the dried dung brickshot like dried dates.[3]

How the same scene keeps getting rewritten may be seen in the *atlal*s of Tarafa and Zuhayr. I quote from yet another translation, this time by the orientalist A. J. Arberry, which keeps close to the originals. First Tarafa:

There are traces of Khaula in the stony tract of Thahmad
apparent like the tattoo-marks seen on the back of a hand;
there my companions halted their beasts awhile over me
saying, "Don't perish of sorrow; bear it with fortitude!"[4]

And now Zuhayr:

Are there still blackened orts in the stone-waste of Ed-Darraj
and El-Mutathallam, mute witnesses to where Umm Aufa once
dwelt?
A lodging where she abode in Er-Rakmatan, that appears
like the criss-cross tattooings upon the sinews of a wrist—[5]

*   *   *

The *Mu'allaqat* approach the condition of song and recall the sinuous cadences played in endless permutations by the Bedouin shepherd on the *shababa*, or reed flute: a single, undulating line offering a multiplicity of choices. Even as the sand sweeps over the desert and effaces every trace of man, a voice ascends in song and asserts its transitory presence in rhythms said to have had their origins in the camel's tread. And what if that voice, the earliest in Arabic poetry, drew repeatedly on the wilderness, on its va-

cant stare, precisely in acknowledgment of a void inherent to being? "For the desert, surely, is one sort of void," Jacques Berque
observed. "And the poet, or his utterance, in the desert is truly
a being endeavoring to situate himself in a negativity no longer
endured but voluntary."[6]

* * *

"Cocooned in her litter," in Jaroslav Stetkeyvich's elegant phras-
ing, the beloved sets out on her journey. "She is the repository of
all the tenderness, and at times playfulness, of *nasib* lyricism and
the poetic topos she generates is classical Arabic poetry's eternal
adieu."[7] Imru al-Qays, as we have seen, gives us the barest outline
of such a scene, but in Zuhayr we are invited to prolong our gaze.
The poet stares hard at the bleak sight of the ruined abode he can
hardly recognize after a twenty-year absence—scraps of stone
waste, the detritus of a long-lost love—and then comes the sudden rush of involuntary, replenishing memory, so palpably real
that the reader remains uncertain whether the poet is reliving his
past or pointing to an actual procession of camels. Again I quote
from O'Grady:

> Look over that way, friend.
> Do you see ladies travelling on high howdahs
> on that high-road above the waterline?
> They will have passed across rough ground to your right.
> How many friends, enemies live there?
> Their howdahs should pile hung with dark damasks
> and finely spun veil transparencies
> with rose-red fringes.
> In their costly clothes they should look coyness personified.
> And the trusses of dyed wool where they alighted
> resemble uncrushed red berries.

At sunrise they stirred. At dawn they rose.
And when they went to the blue water in that brimming well
they stuck their sticks as you'd pitch a tent to stay.
Sweet sight to gentle eyes.
Beauty for who's bound to beauty.[8]

The ladies in their "high howdahs" will not stay. Loyal to the clan, they follow the customs of a nomadic life, pitching for a season their long low tents, which the Bedouin call *bayt al-sha'r*, house of hair, and then bundling their sparse belongings and moving on to new grazing grounds.

The ruined camp triggers a series of bittersweet memories. First comes the fading away, or *ẓaʾn*. To convey a sense of powerful emotion, Imru al-Qays speaks metaphorically of the hard-shelled colocynth,[9] or bitter apple: "Upon the morn of separation, the day they loaded to part, / by the tribe's acacia it was like I was splitting a colocynth." Arberry's version hews close to the Arabic. The prickly umbrella acacia was commonly associated with the pre-Islamic goddess Uzza, while the pulp of the colocynth induced abortions and coarse oil was pressed from its seeds. These specificities (along with their connotative value) are swept aside in O'Grady's version, but what is lost in detail is gained in immediacy:

On the day of departure,
the dawn they loaded to move on,
by those thornbushes
I broke up like burst fruit.

Friends reined in above me.
"Don't break for heartbreak.
Stick tough," they called.
Later, alone, I howled my eyes out at that dark.

What's left to lean together with, longing against
When life's outlines get swept away?[10]

The blurring or erasure of life's outlines—as in a sandstorm—
is what provokes the poet's riposte, which begins with a ribald roll
call of sexual conquest followed by a chivalrous account of the
stations of love. The power of the *nasib* derives from its polarities.
On the one hand, we witness sexual prowess, as epitomized in the
conquest of Unayza, described as "the most indecent verses ever
spoken by an Arab poet";[11] and on the other, a lyrical idealization
of the beloved—exemplified by the figure of Bayda ("egg")—
that would later become a commonplace in the urbane poetry of
the Abbasids, in the Persian *ghazal*, and in the Andalusian strophic
muwashshahat. This idealization may in turn have left its mark on
the troubadours of Provence, whose poems Pound spoke of as
being "a little Oriental in feeling."[12]

Imru al-Qays's amorous exploits ascend the Platonic ladder
of idealized love, beginning with the young girls of Dara Juljul,
for whom he "hacked [his] she-camel,"[13] moving on to Unayza,
to the scornful Fatima, and finally culminating in the drawn-out
splendors of Bayda:

> Then there was Bayda, cloistered in her shell.
>   I had her too, after I'd skirted the tribesmen
> who'd boasted they'd kill me. The Pleiades had just risen
>   and gleamed like gemmed fringes on a sash
> when I entered, and she shivered behind the divider,
>   her clothes there in a heap beside her, except
> for her shift. "By Allah, you won't get away with this!"
>   she cried, as I egged her on and she swept
> our tracks clean with the edge of her brocaded gown.
>   We crossed the campground and dropped
> out of sight in the ribbed hollow of a giant dune,

and when I parted her braids, she leaned forward—
slender-hipped, firm-ankled, slim, egg-white,
   her abdomen flat and breastbones
buffed like a burnished mirror—and shying back
   revealed the softest cheek, the glance
of a Wajra gazelle with its fawn, and an antelope's
   neck, neither uncomely nor unadorned
when raised in full view, and the dark shock of her hair
   curled down her back like clusters of dates
(while her upswept locks were plaited with threads
   lost in a tangle of loosened strands)
and a waist as small as a camel's nose-ring,
   and a shinbone lean as the stalk of a papyrus.
Mornings, crumbs of musk are scattered on her bed
   where she languishes till noon, not bothering
to slip on a gown or sash, and the fingers she raises
   are not coarse, but soft as the sandworms
of Zaby, or tamarisk toothpicks, and evenings
   she illumines the dark as though she were a light
to a hermit at his devotions. On the like of her
   the wise gaze with fervor as she flaunts
her curves in a dress midway between a child's frock
   and a woman's robe. Fresh as an ostrich's
yellow-speckled egg, nourished by unsullied water.
   Other men's follies divert their passions
but my heart won't swerve from loving her,
   and many a pigheaded rival I've repulsed,
sincere, disapproving types, never short of advice.[14]

*　*　*

Early Western theorists of classical Arabic poetry spoke disparag-
ingly of the piling up of seemingly irrelevant detail in the *qasida*;

such vertigo of similes was, as one despairing orientalist claimed, no more than "versified geology and anatomy."[15] But in effect the *qasida*'s technique is cinematic: slow pan, close-up, quick cut, flashback, voice-over. Its vision is complex, working like the eye of the sand lizard. The seeming disjunctions that baffled the early critics now appear to complement modern theories of perception. Kenneth Rexroth's comment on Pierre Reverdy's cubist poetry might also apply to the *qasida*: "It is the conscious, deliberate dissociation and recombination of elements into a new artistic entity made self-sufficient by its rigorous architecture."[16]

✶   ✳   ✱

In 1772, some years before sailing for India and eventually publishing his findings on the linguistic correspondences between Sanskrit, Greek, and Latin, the polymathic William Jones, then only in his midtwenties, dashed off a magisterial essay on Arabic poetry to accompany an early collection of his, cumbersomely titled *Poems, Chiefly Translations from Asiatik Languages, together with Two Essays on the Poetry of Eastern Nations and on the Arts commonly called Imitative*. An incorrigible romantic, Jones could not help seeing the poet-warriors of the *Mu'allaqat* as noble savages, their verse full of an archaic, explosive power.

His enthusiasm for the "ancient simplicity" of the nomads and their terrain was boundless: "Arabia, I mean that part of it, which we call the *Happy*, and which the *Asiatics* know by the name of *Yemen*, seems to be the only country in the world, in which we can properly lay the scene of pastoral poetry. . . . It is observable that Aden, in the Eastern dialects, is precisely the same word with *Eden*, which we apply to the garden of paradise."[17] In keeping with the pastoral mood of his renditions, Jones shifts the region in which the early *qasida* evolved from the inhospitable "Arabia Deserta" of northern and central Arabia to the southern extremity of the peninsula, the fertile "Arabia Felix." Ancient home of the Sabaeans, famed for frankincense, myrrh, and gum resin, the rain-fed terraced hills of Yemen contrasted sharply with the savage wastelands to the north.

Jones's Arcadian setting may sound far-fetched, yet the motif of the paradisal lost garden lies at the heart of the *nasib*, embedded in the poet's sifting over the vestiges of his beloved's encampment and in the ensuing resurgence of memories, which are frequently portrayed in antithetical mood swings and the evocation of opposing states of emptiness and replenishment. Just so, the desolation of the campsite evokes in Imru al-Qays the countermemory of sexual prowess, set forth in a series of vignettes of erotic play and plenitude; the return to an Edenic idyll is figured in purely libidinal terms. In the *Mu'allaqa* of Labid, meanwhile, the stark contrast between the speechless stones of the empty site and the poet-hero's reminiscence of green, sloping valleys is made apparent at the very beginning of the *nasib*. Here we have a wistful backward glance at the briefest, yet most intoxicating of earthly paradises, swathed during the short spring in a carpet of delicate blooms. In pre-Islamic poetry—and perhaps the motif goes further back, to the garden of the Song of Songs and even of *Gilgamesh*—the encampment-cum-ruined-garden suggests at once permanence and evanescence, destruction and restoration. Hence the image of erosion in Labid's *atlal*, "the torrent beds of Rayyan / naked tracings, worn thin, like inscriptions / carved in flattened stones," is soon reversed as the poet recalls the revivifying effects of a sudden shower, when "The rills and the runlets / uncovered marks like the script / of faded scrolls / restored with pens of reed."[18]

In search of fodder for their flocks and camels, tribes crisscrossed the peninsula, the pitching and striking of their low-hung goat-hair tents dictated by climatic conditions and the location of boreholes and watercourses. Winter and spring found them in their natural habitat, the steppes of the Najd, or Inner Arabia, encamped in wadis briefly transformed by rain into aromatic beds of precious herbage. During the long summer months, when the desert turned into a blazing cauldron, they drifted west toward the oases of the Hijaz. But Inner Arabia was the Bedouin's true home, and the *atlal*, the ruined abode haunted by the phantom of the beloved, undoubtedly served as the memory trace of those ephemeral moments suspended between gain and loss, homecoming and dispersion.

＊　＊　＊

From the very first lines, the *Mu'allaqat* abound in place-names, which serve firmly to fix—triangulate, one might say—the *atlal* into place. Did such names serve as guideposts? Was the *qasida*, among other things, a sort of map of the desert? Here, after all, were identifiable landmarks in otherwise blank surroundings. Even after the *Mu'allaqat* came to be treated as relics of an earlier nomadic life, its toponyms remained immensely suggestive as the aural repository of lost origins.

Returning to Imru al-Qays, we read, in Arberry's version, "and let us weep, recalling a love and a lodging / by the rim of the twisted sands between Ed-Dakhool and Haumal, Toodih and El-Mikrat."[19] Ed-Dakhool, according to Adnan Haydar, is derived from the verb *dakhala*, "to enter," which connotes sexual penetration, while Haumal stems from *hamil*, "pregnant," and specifically refers to "clouds black by reason of the abundance of their water." Imru al-Qays locates the *atlal* on an edge or margin, a strip of "twisted sands" running between the desert and the sown, depletion and replenishment. The Arabic term for twisted sands is *bi siqti al-liwa*, and according to Haydar, *siqti* refers to "a child or young one or fetus that falls from the belly [womb] of the mother abortively or in an immature, or imperfect state . . . or dead," and *al-liwa* derives from the verb *lawaya*, "to become withered."[20]

Right from the start, then, contrary modes of being are suggested by the very toponyms: the eviscerated and the life-bearing, their sounds woven into the sand dunes, just as the opposing weave of the south and north winds batters but cannot completely efface the ruined encampment.

*   *   *

It was in spring that the tribes observed the Sacred Month of Peace. The importance of this yearly cessation of strife cannot be underestimated, especially with regard to the sixth century, the time of the great qasidists of the *Mu'allaqat*. Arabia as a political entity, or loose confederation of tribes, was far from being the idyllic dreamland of "ease and leisure" fancied by Jones.[21] The Byzantines to the west and the Persians to the east posed a constant threat to the north of the peninsula. The south, meanwhile, having been invaded by Ethiopians and then Persians, was in the throes of change as ethnic minorities—Monophysites, Syriacs, Jews, and Zoroasters—turned Arabia Felix into a contentious land of rival sects and heresies.

The boundaries between north and south were no longer as clearly delineated as in the past. An increasing number of Arabs from the south migrated north after the bursting of the great dam of Ma'rib, which, according to legend, was the first in a series of catastrophes that led to the depopulation of the country (and to the coining of the proverb "Dhahabu aydi Saba," "They dispersed like the people of Saba"). As South Arabia and its unique script gradually died away the dialect of the north flourished. It was soon to be perfected in the idiom of the *qasida*, which formed the basis of *al-arabiyya*, the common language of the Koran.

As Inner Arabia gained ascendancy its nomadic population came into closer contact with the outside world. The Bedouin began riding out of their hinterlands and offering their services to the great powers to the east and west. When not showing off their equestrian skills and military prowess, they served as cara-vanners to the long camel trains threading northward toward the Fertile Crescent, or westward to the Mediterranean. As a result the Hijaz and Najd were transformed from an "ethnic reservoir," in the words of Irfan Shahid, to an intermediary zone or "transit area."[22] The Bedouin could now choose to lead either a nomadic or a semisedentary life, as the oases of western Arabia became way stations on the trade route, the *via odorifera*.

This period—roughly a hundred years before the advent of Islam—also witnessed a remarkable efflorescence of Bedouin po-etic activity. The *Mu'allaqat* are its showcase pieces, but scores of other poets fill the thirty-three-volume *Kitab al-Aghani*, which, as we have seen, Ibn Khaldun called the compendium of the Arabs, "a witness to the right behavior and their wrongdoing."[23] Antara's depiction of the *atlal* suggests, in fact, that already in the sixth cen-tury the poet felt a certain lack of elbowroom, even in the wastes of Arabia: "Have the poets left a single spot for a patch to be sewn? / or did you recognize the abode after long meditation?"[24] Far from suffering through an "Age of Ignorance"—as *Jahiliyya*, the standard term for the pre-Islamic era, is usually translated—many of these pagan poets were well traveled, wily troubadours, often of noble lineage, who lived at a time of religious and cultural eclecticism.

The authors of the *Mu'allaqat* donned and shed various guises—protector of the tribe, vagabond, soldier of fortune, out-law—as they reaped the benefits, and sometimes paid the penal-ties, of venturing even farther afield. (Zuhayr appears to have been the only one to spend his entire life in Najd.) Imru al-Qays, for instance, is said to have been warmly received in Constantinople by Justinian I, only to be murdered by the emperor by means of a poisoned shirt, supposedly in revenge for the poet's seduc-tion of a princess. Tarafa too wandered the desert in search of patronage and eventually incurred the fatal wrath of a monarch, namely the formidable Amr Ibn Hind, king of al-Hira, who had the poet ambushed and killed for having boasted of a dalliance with the king's sister. It was at the magnificent court of al-Hira as well that Labid's talents as a poet were first recognized, and the aging al-Harith, we are told, cut his hand on the strings of his bow as, overcome by emotion, he recited his *qasida* in front of Amr Ibn Hind. At the king's final encounter with a *Mu'allaqa* author, however, it was he and not the poet who bled: Amr Ibn Kulthum had, according to legend, come to al-Hira to strike the king down in revenge for the murder of Tarafa.

Like the poets themselves, the poems radiated in all directions, and in so doing finely registered their surroundings. Thus Tarafa compares his *naqa* to a Byzantine bridge, her neck to "the rudder [or prow] of a Tigris-bound vessel," her cheeks to "Syrian parchment," and her lips to "a tanned hide of Yemen."[25] The poets' repeated scoring of the vast peninsula on their "silent great shuffle-footed beast[s],"[26] trekking between tribal encampment, oasis, and caravan city and penetrating even into the Fertile Crescent, was not unlike the way the Greek pastoral poets—Theocritus, for instance—plied the Mediterranean, all the while writing poetry at once intensely local and, in its absorption and melding of diverse strands of Greek, cosmopolitan. Bahr bi-la ma' ("sea without water"), the Bedouin sometimes called their desert wilderness, and as we have seen in Tarafa's depiction of Maliki camels tacking across the broad wadi like "great schooners," caravans were frequently compared to seafaring vessels.

*   *   *

How to fully grasp the resonating power of the *nasib*? Loss and reminiscence are undoubtedly embedded in the Bedouin's seasonal migrations; the ruined encampment and the caravan fading into the distance were recurring sights that would have assumed heightened symbolic value over time. Yet one cannot help wondering whether the *atlal* did not also express a larger, more complex vision of dispersion.

Scattered about the Arabian Peninsula, incised in its rocks, are thousands of inscriptions, classified today as Thamudic, Sabaean, Nabatean, Safaitic, or Lihyanic, and dating roughly, it is thought, from 800 BC to AD 400. They seem to be largely shepherds' graffiti and include assertions of identity ("And this is Hadir, drowsy because of illness"), boasts of valor ("Bi-ha-Shirkat gave assistance in the war against Dedan, spying out for Salm"), and declarations of love ("Hslt loves the mouth of Gall" and the far more explicit "And Z'g and Zufray have committed adultery. / And this deed stinks worse than a stinking fart").[27]

Such inscriptions, transcribed by a long line of explorers—Charles Doughty, Alois Musil, Douglas Carruther, St. John Philby, A. J. Jaussen, and R. Savignac—belie the commonly held notion of Bedouin illiteracy before the advent of Islam. What is more, these brief declarations of illness and recovery, love and war, were not the only writings that the poets of pre-Islamic Arabia were bound to encounter during their peregrinations. Also cut into outcroppings were numerous funerary inscriptions; the most famous, written in Nabatean and dating from the fourth century, is dedicated to Imru al-Qays's namesake (though not his ancestor, as the poet's real name was Hunduj):

This is the funerary monument of Imru al-Qays, son of 'Amr, prince of all of Arabia, the one who wore the diadem, who subjugated the [tribes] of Asad and Nizar, as well as their princes, who dispersed Madhhidj to this day, who brought success [?] at the siege of Nadjran, city of Shammar, who subjugated [the tribe] of Ma'add, who put his sons in charge of the tribes and delegated them to the Persians and Romans. To this day no prince has attained such glory. He died the year 223, the 7th of kaslul [December 7, 328].[28]

Such epitaphs cannot but suggest the presence, in the heart of the desert, of a former grandeur, equal perhaps to the ruins of the rock-carved funerary temples of Mada'in Selih and, further north, of Petra.

The nomadic poets of Arabia, I would like to suggest, were well acquainted with these monumental ruins, as they were with the numerous stone sanctuaries, rock drawings, and horizontal, vertical, and even boustrophedonic graffiti scattered about the peninsula. Mute traces of once-flourishing cultures haunted the sand wastes, from the Himyarite kingdom at the southern tip of the peninsula to the Nabatean Empire in the north. How frail, how ephemeral was the material world of the Bedouin! And yet when he looked about, he found that for those who abandoned the desert ethos of frugal subsistence, the glory was illusory and brief.

It follows that the *atlal* should perhaps be read not only in terms of personal loss but as a kind of communal memento mori, a reminder of the ever-present dangers of cultural diminishment and tribal fragmentation, even dissolution, as nomadism was gradually replaced by the sedentary life of towns and oases. It is against this background that we must hear the call of the great qasidists to halt and pause awhile at the deserted campsite.

* * *

Might such a sense of imminent change, even within the seemingly immutable desert scape, explain the *qasida*'s extreme mood swings within and between each of its movements? After the *nasib* comes the devil-may-care plunge of the *rahil*, which quickly moves from reminiscence to action, which Arab critics of the *qasida* called *takhallus*, "disengagement." Imru al-Qays's challenge to the wolf, at the beginning of his *rahil*, is a case in point. Though playing fast and loose with the original (which includes no mention of crucifixion), O'Grady's lively, colloquial rendition excels at conveying the nimble, alliterative music of a fast-talking gamester:

> Many a waterbag of bravura wastrel brother madness
> I've carried as comrades' crucifixion
> and many's the desert valley,
> bare as a donkey's belly,
> I've traversed where the prodigal wolf
> howls over her progeny
> and I howled back:
> "Well, wolf!
> There's two of us in it
> And neither of us making a much of it.
> If cither of us manage a muckle today,
> it's a mickle tomorrow.
> Our tillage turns shallow.
> Our bargains and barter beggar."[29]

Later qasidists give to the hero's journey a specific destination, namely the patron's court, where the poet's final lavishing of praise may be heard. In the *Mu'allaqat*, however, he simply gallops into the desert wastes. Not infrequently the day's journey is preceded by a gloom-filled night passage punctuated by the hooting of an owl. His *naqa* (or sometimes his *faras*, "horse") is now his only companion, and what ensues is a detailed catalog of its features, an obsessive tallying accompanied by ever-widening associations. Some of Tarafa's *naqa* similes have already been mentioned, but he also compares parts of the beast's anatomy to coffin planks, a water bag, the double doors of a fortress, the casing of a vault, a kind of shrub, a water carrier lugging two full pails of water, wedged-in roof beams, and an anvil. Such extended similes reach to the very essence of the creature, man's boon companion ("quickened, compact, / like a stone hammer / against a hardened slab"[30]), the statuesque yielding to the kinesthetic, which in turn yields to the sensory organs: ears, lips, nose, and

> Eyes like two mirrors
> sheltered in the rock
> browbone's caves,
>   two carved-out pools,
>
> Eyes shielded from dust
>   like the two dark ones
>   of a frightened doe oryx
>   with fawn.[31]

The long-necked desert beast, head carried high above the wind-swirled sand, is the protean, transforming agent of the *rahil*. It will frequently trigger, by way of comparison, scenes or episodes involving other desert creatures, such as the ostrich, the sand grouse, the pigeon, the hawk, the wild ass, the gazelle, the antelope, and, notably, in Ladid's *Mu'allaqa*, *al-thawr al-wahshi*, the so-called wild bull. The *naqa* stood for overwhelming cosmic forces as well as for the aesthetic perfection of material culture. Perhaps most significantly, it embodied, in its seemingly contrary attributes, the trials and hardships of the warrior-poet as well as the grace and desirability of the beloved.

The *naqa*, as distinct from its more cumbersome male counterpart, was prized in Bedouin society for the variety of its uses. It was swift; it provided sweet milk (according to Doughty, mothers washed their infants in its urine);[32] and it was even—as we shall see momentarily—an object of ritual sacrifice. Should it outlast its owner, the *naqa* was tethered to his tomb and left to die. Hence in Labid's *Mu'allaqa* we read, "To the shelter of my tent-ropes comes every forewearied woman / starved as a tomb-tethered camel, her garments tattered and shrunk."[33] Precisely because of its overdetermined, symbolic role in the life of the tribe, the *naqa*'s proper name was rarely used in the poetry of the Jahiliyya, and in its stead appear—as with the poet's horse—a wide array of connotative epithets and synonyms.

In the *naqa*-sacrifice scene, which usually occurs toward the end of the *rahil*, the animal is offered up not to any god or spirit but to the tribe itself, as a token of cohesiveness and plenitude in the midst of lack. Labid, perhaps the gentlest and most prudent of the *Mu'allaqat* poets, pledges meat to the poor. Imru al-Qays is irreverently playful as he turns the scene—which appears, atypically, in the *nasib*—into a titillating game of catch as the meat is tossed about by young girls. On the other hand, Tarafa, the most rascally of the seven, fobs off not his own camel but that of an "old stick of a man,"[34] thereby incurring the wrath of the tribe. It is, in Michael Sells's words, a "sacrifice gone wrong,"[35] and Tarafa's ensuing boast is tinged with the anxiety of being misrepresented, and of having his reputation tarnished: "Don't make me a man / whose resolve wasn't my own / who could never replace me / or cast my shadow."

* * *

Deep in the sandy recesses of Wadi Rumm, the hunting of oryx, wild ass, ostrich, addax, onager, and ibex is depicted on boulders. Stick figures pursue their quarry, brandishing lances while perched on spindle-legged, hugely humped camels. Such petroglyphs are the pictorial equivalent of the chivalrous hunting scene in the *rahil*. For it was in hunting and raiding that the Bedouin proved his mettle—this being perhaps the closest equivalent in English to the elusive but all-pervasive Arabic term *muruwwa*, "manliness." Resolution, steadfastness, generosity, nobility of character, loyalty to one's clan and genealogy, and a fierce enthusiasm for life, even in the face of the harsh powers of fate: all these fall under the rubric of *muruwwa*, which yokes qualities of control and foresight—what Sells calls "trail sense"[36]—to a paradoxical impetuousness, an expansive élan, that easily turns into unbridled passion and recklessness. The *qasida*, particularly its second and third movements, was the primary vehicle for expressing, often hyperbolically, such supreme virtues.

Among the *Mu'allaqat* poets, the one who perhaps best encapsulates *muruwwa* is Zuhayr, toward the end of his *rahil*. Meticulous, clear-voiced, terse, the most sententious of the select group, Zuhayr the Moralist, also called Abid al-Shi'r ("The Slave to Poetry"), wrote his great *qasida* after the cessation of war between the tribes of Abs and Dhubyan, which was rumored to have lasted forty years. As spokesman for the tribe of Ghatafan, the poet praises the peacemakers, Harim and al-Harith, and in so doing describes the ritual circling of the Ka'bah—a pagan ceremony existing long before the advent of Islam: "So I swear, by the Holy House about which circumambulate / men of Koraish and Jurhum." He inveighs against the horrors of war, then offers a series of gnomic sayings whose balanced, languid movements are best conveyed in William Jones's eighteenth-century English:

He, indeed, who rejects the blunt end of the lance, *which is presented as a token of peace*, must yield to the sharpness of the point, with which every tall javelin is armed.

He, who keeps his promise, escapes blame; and he, who directs his heart to the calm resting-place of integrity, will never stammer nor quake *in the assemblies of his nation*.

He, who trembles at all possible causes of death, falls in their way; even though he desire to mount the skies on a scaling-ladder.

He, who possesses wealth or talents, and withholds them from his countrymen, alienates their love, and exposes himself to their obloquy.

He, who continually debases his mind by suffering others to ride over it, and never raises it from so abject a state, will at last repent of his meanness.

He, who sojourns in foreign countries, mistakes his enemy for his friend; and him, who exalts not his own soul, the nation will not exalt.

He, who drives not invaders from his cistern with strong arms, will see it demolished; and he, who abstains ever so much from injuring others, will often himself be injured.

He, who conciliates not the hearts of men in a variety of transactions, will be bitten by their sharp teeth, and trampled on by their pasterns.

He, who shields his reputation by generous deeds, will augment it; and he, who guards not himself from censure, will be censured.[37]

Committed to an ethos of tribal survival and moral rectitude, the poet, or *sha'ir*, celebrated in the *qasida* the delicate social fabric of nomadic life, which was constantly under threat. The knowledge of the *sha'ir* ran deep. He was tribal propagandist and encomiast, elegist and lampoonist (which would cost Tarafa his life), arbiter and assessor, but also visionary and soothsayer. His powers were said, in fact, to be allied to those of the *jinni*, or desert demon.

This may explain the *qasida*'s darker, more transgressive side. Time and again, particularly in the *rahil*, the poet-warrior presents himself not only as a clan leader but as a rebel and troublemaker, a reviler, a man on the run or companion to a band of outlaws. When deviance dominates the *qasida*, we have in essence a *su'luk* ("brigand") poem. In fact, I would go so far as to say that the *qasida*'s very vitality lies in its incorporation of *su'luk*-like elements. Consider Imru al-Qays, who though of royal descent was banished by his own father for composing verses, and who for the most part led the life of a fugitive. His night journey, "wolf scene," and description of bedding another man's wife could have come straight out of a *su'luk* poem.

*   *   *

Ending as it does with the *fakhr*, or boast, it has been suggested that like a well-aimed arrow, the *qasida* inevitably sought its mark in the glorification of the poet-hero, who concludes the poem by vaunting his lyric and martial prowess. But the poets of the *Mu'allaqat* talk big in a variety of ways. For them, memory was essentially dual, overlaying personal confession and a tribal vision or mythopoeia. The *qasida*'s fluidity allows for both an individual and a collective voice to be heard, and sometimes, as in Labid's *Mu'allaqa*, personal bragging is replaced by extravagant praise of the clan:

> When the assemblies meet together, we never fail
> to supply a match for the gravest issue, strong to shoulder it,
> a partitioner, bestowing on all the tribe their due,
> granting to some their rights, denying the claims of some
> for the general good, generous, assisting liberality,

gentlemanly, winning and plundering precious prize,
sprung of a stock whose fathers laid down a code for them,
and every folk has its code of laws and its high ideal.[38]

Add yet, for all the cocksureness of the *fakhr*, a profound fatal-
ism lies at the heart of the *qasida*; the poet's bravura is asserted
more often than not in the teeth of death. The *fakhr* tries to shake
off an underlying sense of despondency, already intimated in the
abrupt transition between the *atlal* and the headlong journey into
the desert. Tellingly, the boast frequently comes before, during,
or soon after an evocation of the *maysir*, a ritual lottery played
with notched arrow shafts. Thus Labid's boast is qualified by gratitude in the light of his good fortune:

And many a time I've called for the gambling-arrows, so like
Each to each in shape, to kill a gamblers' slaughtering-beast,
Called for the arrows to choose a barren or bearing camel
Whose flesh was distributed to the poor relations of all;
And the guest and the poor stranger must have thought
    themselves
Come down upon Tabala, whose valleys are ever green.[39]

Consider, for instance, the *fakhr* of Antara's *Mu'allaqa*. Known
as the Black Knight, Antara was born to an Abyssinian slave girl
bedded by his father, and was accepted as a true son of the clan
only after dramatically proving himself in battle. His boast, running to over thirty lines, reads not without irony as a danse maca-
bre, a grim display of courage, which devolves into unconstrained
bloodletting. And yet it is precisely here, "as the whirl of death /
dragged champion after champion down,"[40] that the poet aban-
dons for a moment all posturing and deflects his helpless anguish
onto his mount:

"Antara!" they cried,
their spears like well-ropes
netting the forechest
of my deep black stallion.

I hurled him,
head-blaze and breast-pit,
again and again upon them
until he was shirted with blood.

With forequarters from the spear-fall
twisting away,
he complained to me
through tears and snorting.

Had he known how to speak
he would have protested.
Had he known to use words
he would have let me know.[41]

Cast as they are in the wistful, optative mood, one cannot
help but read these lines, in which the poet-hero is unmanned
by the disarming gaze of his black stallion, as an instance of self-
interrogation: the poet is momentarily caught between eloquence
and painful muteness, defiance and despondency, bloodshed and
the wished-for cessation of strife ("My soul was cured of its sick-
ness / and restored / by the cries of the horsemen, / 'Antara,
on' "[42]), in the *qasida*'s—and the battle's—final moments.

*   *   *

In later centuries, in Damascus and Baghdad and elsewhere, the
kind of clan panegyric seen in Labid's *fakhr* gave way to courtly

compliments as Umayyad and Abbasid poets, writing in the new urban style of *tahbir*, "embellishment," turned the *qasida* into a decorative pendant, its vigorous weave of desert motifs reduced to overrefined filigree. There were of course exceptions—one has only to think of al-Mutannabi, the mocking Abu Nuwas, the great ironist Abu Tamman, of Dhu al-Rummah, who brought about, in Gustave von Grunebaum's apt phrase, "the Indian summer of the classical qasidah,"[43] or the Andalusian Ibn Zaydun, lamenting the fall of Cordoba in the gentlest, most melancholy of *nasib*s. At the time of Ibn Zaydun, *qasida*s were also written in Hebrew by Judeo-Andalusian poets, notably Shmuel HaNagid, Solomon Ibn Gabirol, and Yehuda Halevi.[44]

And yet for the most part, cut off from its natural environment, the *qasida* lingered on as a douceur, a nostalgic gesture to an idealized past. Nomadic life had fostered not only strength of character but also *badaha*, a naturalness and spontaneity, that was becoming increasingly rare. (So much so, in fact, that the "settled" Arab population of Mecca sometimes handed their infants over to be suckled and raised by Bedouin wetnurses, in the belief that the desert would encourage vitality and purity of speech.) The eleventh-century Persian poet Manuchehri goes so far as to equate the vanished age of the pre-Islamic qasidists with the demise of poetry: "Amru'l Qais and Labid and Akhtal and blind A'sha and Qais," reads Basil Bunting's graceful rendition, "Who keened over the bones of dead encampments and fallen tents, / as we mourn for the ruins of poetry and broken rhymes."[45] Not for nothing were the seven poets of the *Mu'allaqat* known as "the pedigree stallions," for they could outrun all others.

Attir

Several of Suleiman's fat-tailed sheep aren't doing all that well. One has a blotched fleece, another has an eye covered with a blue film, and a third has curled up dejectedly in a corner. Clad in faded gray sweatpants and a light windbreaker, Suleiman bin Musa leans against their pen. The dawn air is refreshingly crisp, and to the east foreboding layers of cloud cloak the bare hills. I ask whether it could possibly rain this early in the year. Suleiman smiles and says that in an hour or two I'll be feeling the heat. In the early morning light his stone house, with its outlying shacks of sheet metal, stands out clearly. In one of these shacks lives his eighty-year-old mother, while another is home to a daughter who has temporarily moved back to Attir with two small children after quarreling with her husband. He lives in Hura, the official, state-sponsored Bedouin township some eight kilometers to the west and one of seven such townships in the northern Negev.

Suleiman's wife brings us coffee and poppy-seed cakes on a small silver tray. We greet each other politely. Bareheaded and wearing an ankle-length black dress embroidered with red, she vanishes down the slope and soon returns with two plastic stools. I feel that the slightest of chinks has opened in the veiled diffidence common to Bedouin women, as she allows herself to engage in playful banter with her husband in my presence. Might I be the subject of their talk? You mean to take *him* out with you to graze the sheep? My Arabic, however, is too poor to piece together their animated exchange, and for a moment I feel all too keenly the presumption of my weekly forays out of Jerusalem: what was I doing driving south into the dusty margins of the desert when my ignorance of Bedouin life was so broadly manifest? Admittedly Suleiman's eyes had lit up when I'd confessed my admiration for the pre-Islamic poets of Arabia. But was there any relation to speak of between my own nostalgia for a long-vanished nomadic culture and the current plight of the Negev Bedouin?

I had discovered on a previous visit that my rudimentary knowledge of the language was useful solely as an icebreaker: make a fool of yourself and people immediately feel at ease. Suleiman had to drive off to Hura and so instructed his son, Turc, to shepherd me across the dry gully that cuts through the village, to the hill where his father lives. We found Musa bin Husain twisting rusty wires through a hole in one of the corrugated sheets forming a small pen behind his home. Lean, stooped, and clad in a tattered *jallabiyya*, Musa, at eighty-five, is the village *sheikh*, while Suleiman and a second brother, Salim, are his deputies, or, as Suleiman put it, "his wings." We pulled up some chairs under the shade of a scraggly tree, and before I knew it four of his sons and a half dozen children had joined us in a circle. I tried to get Musa to talk about the past—the Mandate days—when the Al-Ke'an tribe camped further west and grazed their livestock on broad fields that since the midfifties have been farmed by kibbutz Beit Qama. Musa, however, kept returning proudly to the fact that he had sired over thirty children. He extended his arm first to the right and then to the left, indicating the homes of his three wives. "Ya'atik il-afiya," I blurted out—may He give you strength. Musa stared at me. "What did he say?" he asked his sons. "Ya'atik il-afiya, Ya'atik il-afiya," they answered, rolling with laughter. Out of the corner of my eye I couldn't help noticing that the wives of two sons, who at regular intervals had been pouring us sweet tea in small glasses, were equally amused. One of Musa's sons, named Hasan, a schoolteacher in Hura, must have felt that it was now his turn to rile his father: "Why is your *jallabiyya* all ripped and torn?" "What are you talking about?" Musa replied, pointing at me. "Look at his shirt; I bet it isn't worth more than a shekel."

*   *   *

Suleiman has called to his wife, who hurries from the house with a carton of medicine bottles and hypodermic needles. The medicine—penicillin, supplementary vitamins, eye lotion—was bought from the vet in Beer-sheva, where Suleiman must renew his shepherd's license regularly. After injecting two of the sheep and cleaning the eye of the third we're ready to go. Suleiman opens the gate and his flock trots out in a wedge. He asks me to run ahead up the dirt path toward the road leading to Hura and to make flapping sounds with my tongue, *grrrr, grrrr, grrrr*, while he takes the rear, picking up a stiff rubber pipe that will serve him as a goad.

There is a pleasant, if somewhat rude, view of the village from the road. Most of the homes scattered on the flanks of the wadi are made of tin or sheet metal hammered to wood frames, but here and there are squat cinderblock dwellings and even a few homes faced with limestone brought from the quarries near Hebron. Large, rusting, cylindrical water tanks are permanently parked on the barren hillside. And at one entrance to the village stands the hospitality tent, or *shigg*. Its black canvas roof stretched over a rectangular ribbing gives the impression of an old river barge run aground.

The sloping turnoff to Attir, however, is unmarked. Nor does it appear on any Israeli roadmap, for Attir is officially designated one of forty-five "unrecognized" Bedouin villages in the Negev.

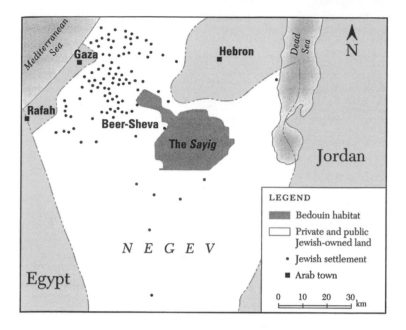

Ranging from some 300 to 4,000 inhabitants, such villages make up half the Bedouin population of the Negev—today numbering 150,000—who over the last thirty years has refused to move from its land. The pressure to do so has come from the Israeli government, which in 1969 initiated the planning and development of Bedouin townships in the northern Negev. This scrubland, the *sayig*, covers a thousand square kilometers where in the early fifties the military had concentrated the dwindled population of the Negev Bedouin—who had by then received, at least technically, full Israeli citizenship, as had Muslim and Christian Arabs living in the north. But one should keep in mind that close to 100,000 Bedouin, 80 percent of the Bedouin populace of pre-state Israel, were expelled or fled to Sinai and Jordan during the 1948 Arab-Israeli War or its aftermath.

First the exodus, and then the displacement and restriction of movement of the remaining tribes came as the coup de grâce in a process begun well over a century ago, during the Ottoman period—referred to by the Bedouin as the "government of the bayonet" (*hukm bi-sanja*)—when large tracts of land in the Negev were declared state-owned. Intertribal warfare began as early as 1799, when the Tiyaha and Tarabin tribal confederations lit out of Sinai and jostled for territorial supremacy, particularly in the fertile northwest regions of the Negev, previously dominated by the Wuhaydat. The Bedouin closed ranks briefly to join the countrywide rebellion against the Egyptian Ibrahim Pasha, who wrested Palestine from the Turks in 1831. The rebellion was quelled, however, and the Pasha got even with the Bedouin by having many of them deported or conscripted into his army. In 1840 the Turks restored Ottoman rule, and rival Bedouin factions resumed the periodic raiding of each other's camps, culminating in the twenty-year-long War of Zari and, close on its heels, the Azazme-Tarabin War (1887–90). The latter was brought to an end only after the Ottoman governor of Jerusalem, Rashid Pasha, dispatched an army to the Negev and "carried off thirteen sheikhs in irons to Jerusalem," as W. M. Flinders-Petrie, a British archeologist excavating at the time near Gaza, would write.[1] The British Mandate period witnessed further upheavals, including the taxation of crops and the continuing penetration from the north of Arab peasants seeking work on the fringe of the Negev. In addition the Jewish Agency began purchasing land in the 1930s from Bedouin chiefs and would soon establish, in defiance of British rule, a handful of Jewish communal agricultural settlements, or *kibbutzim*, in the region.

To the nine tribes that already lived in the *sayig* in the fifties were added eleven tribes whose grazing grounds outside the enclosure were subsequently expropriated by the Israel Land Administration, which is in charge of administering and leasing state-owned land (approximately 93 percent of the land in Israel). Ostensibly the purpose was to provide centralized services such as health care, education, and housing, and in such a way as to narrow the economic and cultural gap between the seminomadic Bedouin and the rest of the Israeli population. Moshe Dayan, minister of agriculture at the time, spoke of the day when "Bedouin children will be accustomed to a father who wears trousers, does not carry a *shabaria* [traditional Bedouin knife] and does not search for vermin in public. The children will go to school with their hair properly combed. This will be a revolution, but it can be done in the space of two generations. Without coercion but with governmental direction . . . this phenomenon of the Bedouin will disappear."[2]

That was in 1963, a time when the entire Arab community in Israel still lived under martial law. Two generations have passed, and as I clamber down the other side of the road into a deep pocket of waste ground along with Suleiman and his 250 head of sheep, I breathe a sigh of relief that the Bedouin have not vanished despite considerable government coercion, though the changes have been profound and frequently traumatic, and Suleiman's gem-studded *shabaria* is no longer fastened to his waist but hangs on the wall of his living-room-cum-*shigg*. His sheep are moving at a slow pace, heads lowered, nuzzling around dry thistles and munching at thin yellow stalks. Suleiman is beaming: this, I am told, is a particularly nutritious patch of land, although all I see are parched weeds. Whenever he watches his sheep grazing bountifully, he confides, he feels he's on his knees eating alongside them. I'm reminded of King Nebuchadnezzar of Babylon, who "did eat grass as oxen."[3] We're moving deeper into the wadi and the skies have cleared to a milky blue, like the filmy eye of Suleiman's ailing sheep now trailing behind the rest of the flock. To the northeast are the rugged West Bank highlands. Closer lies Yattir Forest, planted by the Jewish National Fund as part of its effort to "redeem the land of the Negev," while the round, blurred contours of bare hills to the south hint at the vastness of the desert stretching toward the Gulf of Aqaba. Although sparsely populated, the Negev, shaped like a massive, pressure-flaked arrowhead, covers over half the area of modern-day Israel.

Suleiman recounts how his tribe moved to Attir in the midfifties. Unlike other tribes living outside the *sayig* who were ordered by the military administration to relocate, the Al-Ke'an tribe turned to the Israeli Defense Forces (IDF) as a result of a long-standing intertribal dispute over grazing rights and asked to be moved. Suleiman explains, "We were a small tribe who'd migrated from Arabia some three hundred years ago and had lived for many years under the protection, *fi batan*, 'in the stomach,' as we say in Arabic, of the Al-Huzayil. By the 1940s our tribe had grown and my father asked the Al-Huzayil tribal council to be released from their protection. We no longer want to be *fi batan*, he said, leave us alone. But once we were on our own, word spread that we weren't true Bedouins, since we'd lived for years under the protection of the Al-Huzayil, and it was only in 1980—when one of our members went on a Hajj to Mecca and traced our ancestry there—that we were able to prove our lineage. In 1956 we asked to leave Beit Qama, where we'd dug a well, and the army set us marching eastward. I know it was 1956 because that happens to be the year I was born. In fact I was born during the journey. We stopped in a field right after the Shoket junction and my mother gave birth. The Israeli commander came up to my father and asked, 'Why have you stopped?' and he told him, 'My wife has just given birth to a son.' That night my father slaughtered seven sheep, for I was the firstborn boy after six girls. When we got to the wadi where we now live, the commander gave my father an old assault rifle and told him to keep an eye on the Jordanian border for infiltrators."

Suleiman recalls how his father had been shot in the leg while they were grazing sheep along the demarcation line. He thinks it was a Jordanian from the village of Samu'a who hoped to scare off the pair and steal their herd across the border. Theft and the smuggling of livestock were fairly common. This was a time when thousands of Palestinians, refugees from 1948, recrossed the border illegally every year, seeking lost property and relatives, or merely wishing to reap the harvest in their abandoned fields. But armed bands also slipped across the armistice line intent on raiding remote settlements, and the IDF, shooting first and asking questions later, showed little tolerance for any form of incursion.[4] Suleiman, six years old at the time, remembers getting his wounded father onto his donkey and riding back to their encampment, where his cousins squeezed Musa into a beat-up Dodge, the only car in the village, and drove off in a cloud of dust to the nearest hospital in Beer-sheva.

*　*　*

We reach a low stone outcropping. Suleiman unzips his windbreaker and spreads it on the ground for me to sit on. Several weeks ago the area was declared off-limits by the IDF, and Suleiman had to herd his sheep elsewhere as the wadi droned with tanks and half-tracks on maneuvers. But he is unfazed by the military. They come and go; and once they're gone he's back grazing on his favorite terrain, with its two tall trees planted by his uncles in 1956 and its deep ravine incongruously lush in the otherwise parched landscape. But what does worry Suleiman endlessly are the ILA and the Ministry of the Interior. Representatives of the latter beefed up by police and the notorious Green Patrol—a paramilitary unit set up in 1976 by Ariel Sharon, then minister of agriculture, to patrol the Negev—descended on Attir last July and served the villagers four demolition orders, including one for Suleiman's home. "The government put us here in 1956 and now they're trying to force us to move to Hura so they can build a Jewish town on the ridge behind Attir."

Coercion—or as Dayan put it, "direction"—on the part of the government has meant withholding from all the unauthorized villages such services as running water, electricity, sewage, roads, and public transportation. Coercion has also involved the constant threat of house demolition (any structure with a cement floor and cinderblock or stone walls), a threat which has been stepped up since Sharon—nicknamed "the bulldozer" by Jews and Arabs alike—took office. Crops grown on land the state considers its own have been routinely plowed over, and in the last two years close to twenty thousand *dunam*s of "illegally grown" crops have been destroyed by the aerial spraying of a herbicide (redoubtably called Roundup). Sharon, who owns a large sheep farm in the Negev, has criticized the Bedouin for "seizing new areas and eroding the state's last reserves of land."[5] For years the official position has been that Jewish agricultural settlements and bedroom communities must go up in the northern Negev as a means of curbing the sprawl of Bedouin shanties, even though the Bedouin, making up 20 percent of the Negev population, live on only 2 percent of the land.

Yet the Israeli authorities seem less concerned about the social and economic needs of the Bedouin population than about the perceived demographic threat. With one of the highest birthrates in the world, it is only a matter of time before the spreading Bedouin population will serve as an uninterrupted "Arab presence" across the narrow waist of the Negev that separates the West Bank and Gaza. And although the Bedouin are, as mentioned earlier, Israeli citizens, and many have served as trackers in the IDF, their loyalty to the state continues to be questioned.

On one of my visits to the Al-Ke'an tribe I drove up a long, bumpy dirt road that led to a lone farmhouse—actually no more than a decrepit shack with a sagging porch—worked by a Jewish couple. Amos, an electrical engineer by training, left Beer-sheva in 1990 and settled on six thousand *dunam*s of land leased from the Lands Authority. Living conditions weren't that different from those of his Bedouin neighbors: a generator provided electricity, and water was piped in from Hura. A horse and two mules rubbed their flanks against the small corral in front of his home. There was also a sheep pen, but I gathered that most of Amos's income came from raising bulldogs and servicing generators in the West Bank settlements. "So why live here?" I asked. "The air's good here, I don't have any neighbors, and besides," he added with a touch of pride, "someone has to hold onto the land."

"What do you mean?"

"Look around, they're spreading everywhere, living scot-free on state land."

"You mean the Bedouin?"

"Of course the Bedouin. They marry women from the West Bank who don't even raise their children as Israelis. They don't work and the only reason they have so many children is to collect their child allowance. And they claim the Negev belongs to them. Look at aerial photographs from the thirties and forties; you won't see any Bedouin, they only show up when there's an Israeli settlement they can live off or steal from. I'll tell you something, they call the Bedouin the sons of the desert, but they're actually the fathers of the desert: wherever they settle the land turns into a desert."

*   *   *

Suleiman pulls a thermos out of his knapsack and pours Turkish coffee into two small glasses. "So why not move to Hura?" I ask him. "It's only eight kilometers away; you could build yourself a two-story stone house and even keep a sheep pen in the backyard and bales of hay, like the other residents of Hura." Suleiman twirls a short dried stalk of flax between his fingers. He confesses to owning two lots in Hura, bought in 1989 when the township was founded. At the time three Abu Al-Ke'an clans agreed to move there. It was only his grandfather's clan who decided to stick it out in the hills, and that clan is now dispersed in loose clusters of tents and shacks along the twelve-kilometer stretch between the township and the lower slopes of the Hebron mountain range, where the 1967 border once ran. But despite countless inquiries at the Beer-sheva office of the government-appointed Administration for the Advancement of the Bedouin in the Negev—the ILA-affiliated agency in charge of Bedouin land claims, known as the *minhelet*—he has never been able to ascertain the whereabouts of his two *dunam*s of land.

Located in cramped quarters above the yellow neon sign of the Golden Geese restaurant on the outskirts of the city, the *minhelet* is, as one official told me, the carrot to the rod wielded by the Ministry of the Interior: the ministry is in charge of issuing demolition orders for illegal house construction, while the *minhelet*'s aim is to work out a compromise with each and every Bedouin family still living outside the townships. Ideally each household would be compensated financially for land and property loss, and offered a plot of land at a reasonable rate in one of the official townships. The ILA, moreover, intends to develop new townships that, at least on paper, are planned as model communities. For the Bedouin, however, the task of demarcating land claims is fraught with internal tensions caused by disputes between families and clans over land parceling. Moreover the thought of living in a planned township has little appeal in light of the chronic dysfunction of the existing townships, which suffer from rampant unemployment, crime, and drug abuse, and which are populated largely by *fellaheen* Bedouin. The *fellaheen* were originally peasants from the north and center of Palestine who migrated south at the turn of the twentieth century in search of employment, gradually adapting Bedouin garb and customs and even acquiring semi-Bedouin status. And yet, not having any true blood or territorial claims, they are regarded to this day as inferior by those Bedouin boasting Arabian descent. Living in the same township, even if in different neighborhoods, has been a source of constant friction between the two groups, at times ending in violent clashes. And in spite of the *minhelet*'s avowal that the new townships will be planned according to individual tribal needs, most Bedouin remain deeply skeptical of the government's intentions.

"They probably sold my plots to someone else as well," Suleiman remarks. "Anyway, I'm not planning to move. The simplest solution is to recognize our village so that we can go on living here as we have for the last forty years. You know what my identity card has for my home address? The name of our tribe, Abu Al-Ke'an. I don't even have an address, because the homes you see don't exist as far as the government is concerned. Three of my brothers teach in Hura, another brother has a furniture shop there, and a cousin of mine, a tile factory. But when they finish work they all return to Attir—even if it means, as it did till three years ago, coming back and sweltering under a tin roof."

I ask Suleiman why the clusters of villages along the road from Hura are all made up of tin structures, while there appears to be a boom of modest-looking stone and cinderblock homes in his own wadi. Five years ago, he explains, in October, a storm raged through the village and destroyed most of the shacks. Zinc roofs and tattered sacking flew in every direction. But worst of all, three young girls, two of them nieces of his wife, were swept away by the torrent that streamed through the gully. Their bodies were found the next day on the outskirts of Beer-sheva, where the riverbed empties onto the floodplain. A week later Sharon (who in his various ministerial guises keeps popping up like a jack-in-the-box in the checkered history of Bedouin-Jewish relations), serving at the time as minister of infrastructure, arrived on a condolence visit and told the villagers that they should build permanent homes. "He gave us his word," Suleiman adds. " 'Go ahead and build yourselves homes,' he said, 'you don't want something

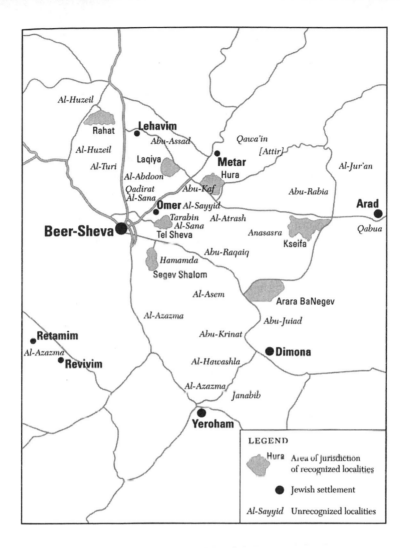

like this to happen again. I promise you it'll be okay.'" Suleiman
and his relatives took Sharon at his word and have been building
ever since: several yards away from Suleiman's own home are two
box-shaped one-room homes nearing completion: one for his aging mother, the other for one of his sons. Across the wadi Yahya,
his eldest son from his first wife, who works as a gardener in Tel

Aviv and has four daughters, is building his own home on a rise hard by the low tin shack where he has lived with his family for the last eight years.

"But what if he breaks his word—surely you're aware of Sharon's reputation," I say.

"I know, but among the Bedouin a man's word is binding."

I remind Suleiman of Sharon's much-publicized Five-Year Plan for the Bedouin, which called for improving the deplorable conditions of the current townships, the construction of seven new towns, and the razing of what government officials call the remaining *pzoura*, or "dispersion," of shanty towns on state-owned land, including Attir. He shrugs his shoulders, whether in resignation or defiance I can't tell. All he sees—he says—are people moving *out* of the townships, giving up their homes in order to move back into shanties on the periphery of the overcrowded and impoverished urban settlements. A Bedouin wants to see the horizon, not the walls of his neighbor's house. (Or, as the school principal in the township of Tel Sheva put it to me, rapping his knuckles on his desk as he spoke, "A Bedouin desires three things: open space, a fast horse, and an obedient wife.") Suleiman recounts how he studied welding in a vocational school in the north of Israel, since there were no high schools for the Negev Bedouin population in the seventies. It was there—in the Galilee—that he acquired his fluent, colloquial Hebrew. He has worked everywhere—Tel Aviv, the coastal plain, Beer-sheva—and earned decent wages, but what he likes best is to herd his sheep in the wadi fanning out on the other side of the pitted road that leads to and from Hura.

I'm startled by the muffled singsong tones of a mobile phone coming from Suleiman's knapsack. After an animated exchange in Arabic peppered with Hebrew catchwords and phrases—a common phenomenon among many male Bedouin—Suleiman snaps the cell phone shut. He smiles. "If you're not connected to the world, the world forgets you." We round up the flock, casting stones at a couple of sheep that have strayed. It was one of his young cousins who had called. His wife had taken their daughter and returned to her family a couple of weeks ago. But now that she's ready to come back, her husband is causing problems: he wants Suleiman to tell her not to bother. "If you have more than five daughters, like I have, then you're considered an Abu Banat, someone that the tribe can turn to in settling marital or family problems," Suleiman explains.

"So what happens next?"

"I try to talk sense into him." Suleiman relishes his role as a counselor, and not only to his own tribe. Twice a week he drives to Beer-sheva in his white Mazda and volunteers at the Welfare Department, counseling the Bedouin. He has also attended courses at the Adler Institute for Family Counseling and hopes to set up a program in Hura on parenthood and child rearing.

* * *

For the Bedouin, courtship, marriage, and the division of labor in the family follow strict patterns, all to the male's advantage. Suleiman admits as much and would like to see some changes, but at the same time feels protective regarding the Bedouin woman's traditional role in the family, which, he adds, can best be safe-guarded by the tribe, living within its own *dira*, or territorial boundaries. He himself has three wives and has fathered twenty children. His first wife moved back to Jordan after they divorced. I haven't yet met his second wife, but Suleiman tells me that she lives in the village. I had heard that many divorced or separated Bedouin wives chose to continue living in the former husband's village in order to stay close to their children, who, according to Bedouin custom, remain with the father after a divorce. "Sure, we're in touch," he responds to my prodding, "but most of the time I live with Salma." How did he and Salma meet? Suleiman describes paying frequent visits to a cousin's *shigg* in a hamlet a kilometer down the road. He'd catch glimpses of her sitting behind the partition in the woman's section and felt drawn to her. "The next step," he explains, "is to get your mother to visit the girl's family on some sort of excuse, like bringing eggs or a chicken, and then have her spy on the girl. She doesn't talk to her, but just looks and forms an impression."

"Then what?" I ask as we lag behind the flock, where heads are raised high, smelling the path home in the warm air.

"My mother spoke to my father. She liked Salma, so all that was left was for my father and one of his brothers to visit Salma's father and declare my intentions. Salma's father told my father to come back in two weeks."

"Did he consult with Salma?"

"Sure, and in our case we even met, once, for about an hour, in the *shigg*."

"And she liked what she saw?"

"Yes, but the truth is she'd noticed me before. And her father approved because of my standing in the village—that counts for a lot."

"What would have happened if she had said sorry, but no?"

Suleiman laughs. "He'd probably have tried to exert some pressure, but in the end the decision would have been hers to make."

"Is that typical?" I ask.

By way of answer Suleiman tells me about a young couple from Hura who had married against their parents' wishes and fled to the center of the country, living in hiding for a number of years before their families were finally reconciled to their union. "But there are," he adds, "less happy endings." I knew that intertribal blood feuds could be fierce, and that such tensions often surfaced in the townships where boundaries between rival tribes were no longer operative. In the case of Suleiman's own son, however, there had been an unexpected reversal of circumstances. Eight years ago, while traveling in Jordan, Suleiman had received a phone call. "Your son has kidnapped our daughter," the voice said in Hebrew on the other end of the line. "That's impossible," he replied, and hastened back to Israel, where he discovered that Yahya had brought home a Jewish girl from Tel Aviv. Far from being abducted, Rita had fallen head over heels for Yahya, and to her parent's consternation agreed to live with him in his village. On first telling me about his daughter-in-law, Suleiman had claimed that her parents were from Poland, but I later found out from Rita herself that she was a second-generation Israeli whose grandparents had come from Thessalonica.

*   *   *

Rita and I first met in August. Pointing to where a bulldozer was leveling the ground near his son's home, Suleiman had suggested I walk over and talk to him. I slipped down the ravine, bypassed the skeleton of a flat-bottom truck snarled in a bend of the dry riverbed, and slowly made my way up the opposite slope. Yahya, a white *kafiyyah* wound tightly around his head, ushered me into his future home. He was a huskier, more exuberant version of his father, and every now and then dashed out of the house and waved at the bulldozer as he barked instructions. The home was nearing completion and, with its three bedrooms, spacious living room, kitchen, and porch, could have passed for a modest villa. We sat on a mattress and talked. He spoke warmly of friends in Tel Aviv and heatedly of the authorities who were threatening to raze his home before he'd even had a chance to move in. When the border police had descended on the village and issued him a demolition order, he walked up to the commanding officer, stuck out his neck, and pointed to his jugular: "Destroy my house," he'd said, "and see if the blood doesn't come spurting out of my vein."

Yahya sprinted out again, and I trailed after him in the sun. We stacked some bales of hay, and then he led me into the shack standing on the edge of the ravine, where he'd been living with his family for the last eight years. There were two windowless rooms, an old crib, and some broken-down furniture. A woman stepped out of the shadows and was introduced as Rita. She smiled faintly and returned to the back of the room, which served as a kitchen. As we were leaving it dawned on me that I'd just been introduced to Yahya's wife. For a second I had been fooled—by her reticence and her Bedouin-style long-sleeved, ankle-length dress—into thinking that she was one of Yahya's sisters or cousins. But Rita had simply been following the custom of a Bedouin woman that forbids her speaking to a male stranger. Would he mind if I spoke to his wife, I asked Yahya nervously. He stared hard at me for a moment, and then smiled and said, "Go ahead, ask her whatever you want." He waved me back into the shack and strode off to have a word with one of the workers.

Rita was startled to see me. Her husband, I explained, had consented to my asking her some questions. "What do you want to know?" she responded. The room filled with children. Minutes later one of Suleiman's teenage boys entered and sank to the floor, absorbed in punching the buttons of his Nintendo. I suspected he had been sent to act as chaperon. Rita spoke haltingly, leaning against the kitchen partition. Since moving to Attir she'd visited her parents once, about five years ago. In the last year, however, she occasionally spoke to them on the phone. She had worked as a bank teller before meeting Yahya. She had a twin sister whom she hadn't seen in eight years and believed was abroad, and a younger brother who was in the army. Her answers were vague and short. Life was hard. She rarely left the village, and only if accompanied by her husband. The day went by swiftly in taking care of her four small girls. Her only company was the other women of the village, who visited frequently and would spend long hours with her, chatting and sharing the household chores. She smiled shyly and lifted her youngest daughter into her arms as the child knocked over a bottle of water and burst into tears.

*   *   *

Two weeks later I returned to visit Suleiman and found Yahya lounging in the living room with his father. Yahya spoke of his and Rita's courtship. All had gone well until Rita's parents heard of their marriage plans. The door then slammed on Yahya, and Rita was confined to her home—"locked up," in Yahya's words—for six months. The pair spoke on the phone, however, and decided to elope. All ties with Rita's family were severed until a year later, when Yahya called her parents to announce the birth of a daughter. They met for the first time in the maternity ward, and Rita's mother lit into him. "She screamed her head off, and in the end I picked up and left." Yet the next day, to his utter stupefaction, Rita's mother greeted him warmly in the hospital and introduced him to the rest of the family. Things went smoothly for the next two years, although Rita's family still refused to visit Attir. But then an Israeli film director shot a television documentary about the Bedouin. Rita was interviewed and made no effort—probably in all innocence—to hide her identity, unlike the other Bedouin women, whose faces were shown blurred. Since then her parents have refused to see her, but they have continued, curiously enough, to maintain ties with Yahya, who drops in on them whenever he's working in the neighborhood.

Yahya is a bit of a wild card. He was married at fifteen to a Bedouin woman and divorced a year later. All a husband has to do is proclaim "I divorce you" three times in front of his wife, and the marriage is annulled. Customarily the wife would then return to her family and tribe, and she could remarry after a period of three months. But as mentioned earlier, many Bedouin women are constrained to remain in a state of limbo, officially divorced from their husband and yet living near him, as a sort of appendage to the family. Since polygamy is illegal in Israel, a husband will at times go through the motions of a divorce simply to introduce a new wife into his household while remaining on the right side of the law. Although divorce can only be initiated by the husband, it is not uncommon for an unhappily married woman to flee—as I had seen in the case of one of Suleiman's daughters—to her father's home for protection. The father or "protector"—Abu Banat, a title Suleiman himself had proudly professed to hold—is then obliged to approach the husband and act, in essence, as a marriage counselor. Sometimes, at the woman's insistence, this might even mean persuading the husband to grant his wife a divorce.

Suleiman, reclining on a mattress next to Yahya, explained that it was his son's early arranged marriage that had made him think twice about interfering with Yahya's choice of a second wife. This time he was going to let his son make his own choices. As it turned out it was a good marriage, and he respected Rita for embracing the Bedouin way of life. But Suleiman was concerned that Yahya, having four daughters but no son from Rita, might seek a third wife, and he worried about the effect this could have on Rita. Yahya remained silent for a minute and then admitted that he did have someone in mind as a third wife. "She's also Jewish, in fact she's ultra-Orthodox and the daughter of a rabbi." For the moment, he told us, she's just a friend, as is her father, who assured him that his home would remain standing since he prayed every day against its demolition. It appears that Yahya's good looks, charm, and desert birthright have won him many a conquest. There was the blond American in Eilat who begged him to return to the States with her, and there were "loose" women in Tel Aviv, and an ultra-Orthodox girl in Jerusalem whose father accused him of violating his daughter and had him arrested. Yahya concluded, "But the girl arrived at the police station and couldn't stop sobbing and kissing me, so the police released me and arrested the father for threatening to kill his daughter."

Listening to Yahya was disconcerting. He was clearly a traditionalist when it came to Rita, but a libertine outside the home. I shuddered at the thought of what would happen to Rita if and when he did bring home a new wife, whatever her origins. He claimed that he'd spoken to Rita and that she had no objections, but in the same breath he told me how everything—a woman's happiness and sorrow, her freedom and responsibilities—were in the hands of her husband. To my surprise Suleiman had argued with his son against bringing another woman into his home. It wasn't only a question of Rita's response. From his own experience he could assure his son that having two or more women under the same roof just didn't work. Times had changed, and women had different expectations. His own second wife left a year after Salma moved in. "And the same happened with the other women," he added. "What other women?" I asked. "I thought you had three wives." Suleiman smiled. "Well, actually I had six wives, but the other three were for very short periods, so they don't really count."

Later that day I trudged up the dirt path leading to Yahya and Rita's new home on the other side of the ravine, hoping to get another chance to talk with Rita. Her nature eluded me. "Who is Rita?" I had jotted down in my notebook. How was it that she had "given up everything," as Suleiman had put it admiringly—her family in Tel Aviv, her friends, her job—to live with Yahya and seemingly accept with equanimity the Bedouin woman's predicament? Since my last visit some of that burden, certainly the physical discomfort of living in a shack, had been alleviated by the move to their new home, even if the windows and doors had yet to be fixed into their frames and only the first five steps leading up to the roof had been completed.

But Rita would remain as elusive as ever on my second visit. As I entered her and Yahya's home I caught a glimpse of her, feeding her children around an old Primus stove in the kitchen and shuffling in and out of the empty rooms before vanishing again, only to reappear briefly with a tray of sweet tea. It was then, however, that Rita spoke in the faintest of whispers, almost as an afterthought to her husband's words, though the irony in her voice left its mark. Yahya had been speaking, a touch dramatically, of their prospects of holding on to their new home. His lawyer had explained to him that implementation of the demolition order was inescapable. All he could do was buy some time. A month, perhaps even a year might pass, but in the end the bulldozers would come—and to add insult to injury Yahya would be required by the state to cover the cost of the demolition. But the honest truth, Yahya then told me, was that he had no objection to moving to Hura. It was a young town, and life would be a lot easier. He was stuck out here "in the middle of nowhere," he claimed, because the village elders in charge of negotiating their terms of compensation with the *minhelet* officials kept making demands that could never be met by the authorities. I foolishly lamented the view they'd be missing by moving to town, at which point Rita spoke up for the first time. "We can have a view of the desert from Hura as well," she murmured, and slipped back indoors.

*　*　*

As we cross the road a car brakes to a halt and lets the last of Suleiman's sheep file pass its fenders. The driver leans out the window and waves to Suleiman. We're now out of last week's military zone and on home ground. Several years ago the Jewish

National Fund planted a large grove of acacias along the ridge leading into the village as part of its ongoing efforts to roll back the desert. The more saplings that were planted and taking root, the less runoff water there would be to erode the soil. The pods of the thorny acacia, I soon learn, provide extra nourishment for Suleiman's sheep. As we enter the grove he raises his rubber goading stick and thrashes away at the branches ("What is that, Moses, thou hast in thy right hand?" reads *surāh* 20 of the Koran. "Why, it is my staff," said Moses, "I lean upon it, and with it I beat down leaves to feed my sheep"). The pods shower down, and within seconds Suleiman's sheep are busy crunching them.

Salma and five of her youngest children, three boys and two girls, are in the large sheep pen, sweeping dung into piles that then get shoveled into burlap bags and removed from the pen by wheelbarrow. They pause as the flock trots determinedly through the gate. Despite three hours of grazing, their hunger seems unabated. One of Suleiman's sons herds the lambs into their own cordoned-off section of the pen. The others head for the water trough, and minutes later, at the sound of barley seeds being poured into a second long metal trough, they huddle forward for their final course of the morning. It is 9 a.m. Cleaning the pen takes at least another half hour. Salma has brought a stiff-haired brush and is vigorously scouring the inside of an empty trough set in the middle of the pen. She silently hands me for safekeeping the white *kafiyyeh* that keeps slipping off her hair as she bends over the trough. I hold the headdress gingerly in my hand as though it were a tiara.

By ten we're sitting in the shade of Suleiman's front porch. Unperturbed by the demolition order he had received in July, he has extended the porch and even added an outdoor sink. Water is pumped to the sink from a tank behind the house, but since the devastating storm of 1997 the village receives a limited amount of water from the National Water Carrier, conveyed aboveground in what looks like narrow-gauge garden hoses. Suleiman's home is also one of the few in the village that has a septic tank. Otherwise villagers simply walk out into the hills to relieve themselves where they can't be seen. I remember how once, while talking to Suleiman's relatives, one of his half-brothers darted into his shack and returned with a transistor radio. "I'm going for a shit," he announced before sauntering off in the direction of the acacia grove. The ethnologist Clinton Bailey, who has recorded the poems recited by Bedouin in Sinai and the Negev, cites one that ends with an allusion to the Bedouin proverb "He who has no land will shit in his hand." The poem, composed in the early forties, castigates a number of Bedouin chiefs for selling their land to the Jewish Agency. The last four couplets in Bailey's translation read:

Look at Ibn Sa'id and Rabi'a, O my!
   They've built houses of stone, painted red and so high!

They've wed daughters of peasants who spice spoiled meat
   And spurned those whose fathers spice coffee-pots.

Their wives stand around in a thin chemise gown,
   Fried foods and soft bread are their only renown.

Even Zirbawi this life couldn't abide,
   When, after shitting, it stuck to each side.[6]

Suleiman brings out his favorite book, *Kalila and Dimna*, and recounts how the animal fables were translated from the Persian in the Middle Ages but go back even further, to ancient India. While I'm admiring the book's cover, depicting two rogue foxes in a not-unfamiliar landscape of rocks and sandy tussocks, Salma serves us bitter coffee. Later Suleiman wants me to take a look at his entire library. I follow him into the kitchen, where he opens a metal cabinet and pulls out a dozen books, for the most part dealing with geography and history. Salma has been preparing two bowls of *ful* and hummus for us, and urges us to return to our seats on the porch. Soon their eldest daughter comes out with a large silver tray laden with food—hummus and *ful*, tomatoes, hot peppers, lentil soup, and piles of paper-thin flatbread called *sajj*. *Sajj* is traditionally cooked on a convex metal plate set over a wood fire, but today most Bedouin use a butane-heated plate. Suleiman invites his wife to sit with us. The children crowd around, giggling. I compliment Salma on the food. She answers in halting Hebrew, but won't venture more than a few words.

*   *   *

A Bedouin buttonholed me on one of my visits south and recounted his favorite tale, struggling to remain poker-faced. A man goes out into the field to relieve himself. Inadvertently he kicks a bottle in the sand, and out comes a *jinni*, who asks him to make three wishes. The Bedouin ponders for a moment and says, "I'd like a donkey." "Okay," says the *jinni*. "What else?"

"A ladder."

"Yes, and what is your third wish?"

"A toad."

"Why on earth would you want a donkey, a ladder, and a toad?" asks the *jinni*. "It's simple," says the Bedouin. "I need a donkey to travel on, a ladder to mount the donkey, and a toad to croak, *crkk*, *crkk*, *crkk*, to get the donkey moving." I didn't make too much of the story at first—supposedly the yarn shows how few are the Bedouin's needs—but now I have begun to think that perhaps its self-deprecating humor and its narrative of diminishing mobility are especially relevant to the plight of the Bedouin in the Negev, though who knows whether the Bedouin of Sinai (whose tribal territories once extended into the Negev), Jordan, and Arabia do not find themselves in a similar predicament?

Having lived traditionally as nomads on the periphery of society, the Bedouin are left with precious little space in which to thrive—culturally, socially, or economically. Whatever the depredations of Ottoman and British rule, in the last fifty years, Israeli statehood and the implementation of wrongheaded, strong-armed policies, coupled with the inevitable expansion of urban communities—modern Beer-sheva, founded by the Turks in 1903 to service the Bedouin population, is now a sprawling city of close to 200,000 residents—the lives and tribal mores of the Bedouin have unraveled at an accelerated pace. They have changed from being pastoral nomads, both tilling the soil and grazing the land, to their present paradoxical condition of *sedentary* nomadism, living for the most part in straitened circumstances on a fraction of the land they once roamed freely. The low-slung hospitality tent pitched behind tin shack or stone home may very well bespeak the ghostly vestige of a life of wandering. That life has turned into the husk of a memory. It is not without significance that when a Bedouin speaks of god-given good fortune, he uses the term for spaciousness (*wusa*), whereas the word for confinement (*dig*) is synonymous with bad luck. Hence the poignancy of the tale in which the make-do of a ladder substitutes for the desert ethos of prowess, while the age-old seasonal migration to pasture and water on horseback and she-camel—the mighty *naqa*, whose long neck is described by Tarafa as a ship's prow rising out of the Tigris—is replaced by the immobility of a donkey barely coaxed into motion by the croaks of a toad.

* * *

I'm invited into the living room, shaped and furnished like a miniature *shigg*, for a last glass of tea before leaving. Mattresses and embroidered pillows are spread on the floor, and Koranic inscriptions in gold and silver calligraphy hang on the walls. We remove our shoes and recline comfortably on our sides, our arms supported by a leaning tower of pillows. Salma enters with a pair of white Nike socks. She and Suleiman both giggle as she leans against his raised feet and struggles to put the socks on properly. "I'd love to herd your sheep with you again," I tell Suleiman. "So you'd better come back soon," he replies. "I'm planning to sell most of them." I wonder if I have heard right. Suleiman explains, "Holding on to the flock is costing me way too much."

"So what will you do instead?"

Suleiman sits up, "I'm thinking of opening a shoe store in Hura."[7]

Notes from Wadi Rumm

. . . whose traces haven't yet been swept away
By the weavings of the southern and the northerly winds

Imru al-Qays

The minibus from Aqaba jolts to a stop. Sliding the side door open
I practically tumble out of the crowded backseat. A tethered camel
baring its teeth stands where the road fades into the gravel plain
at the far end of the corridor separating the sandstone massifs of
Umm Ishrin and Rumm. I enter the modest Government Rest
House, which serves as an information center, restaurant, and
souvenir shop. Pup tents, pitched behind the Rest House building,
can be rented for four *dīnār*s a night, a mattress and blanket on the
roof for two. By nine I'm hiking up to the ruins of the Nabatean
temple, which squats on a slight rocky elevation at the foot of
Jebel Rumm, some five hundred meters behind the campgrounds.
Père Savignac, exploring Wadi Rumm in the 1930s, found the
tail of a bronze dolphin in the temple ruins. He also uncovered
the lower part of a sandstone statue of an enthroned Atargatis,
a favorite Nabatean fertility or grain goddess. Ceres' Levantine
twin sister? Strangely the dolphin motif is not uncommon in this

ancient desert culture: before leaving Jerusalem I'd read of a stone relief of Atargatis found in a lone sanctuary deep in the desert fastness southeast of the Dead Sea, in which the goddess sports a tiara crowned with two baby dolphins.

Vestiges of an old Muslim burial site abut the sanctuary, no more than a scattering of oblong stones, strewn at all angles. I follow a rudimentary map of the area to Wadi S'bach, crossing several narrow ravines before reaching a spring surrounded by fig trees with newly sprouted leaves. Is it the tenacity and transience of desert flora that marshals its colors so? White broom. The tiny field marigold. Low-lying shrubs release a sweet fragrance into the air when I brush against their leaves. A flat sandstone boulder will do as a seat so I can wriggle my toes in the faint morning breeze and squint at the west face of Jebel Mayeen rising above the ramshackle Bedouin village of Rumm. A troop of floppy-eared black goats appears out of nowhere and scrambles up to the spring, nosing into the bone-white shrubs.

A steep ascent. Then down into another dry riverbed. Hard on the knees. I'm out of drinking water, and not a soul in sight. Finally I reach the lower slopes of Wadi Sid. Three Bedouin are lounging under the lip of a huge boulder. I nod in their direction and stride on with the nonchalance of the solitary walker, though just three hours ago I'd been relishing an early-morning bun in the bustle and fumes of Aqaba's central bus station. Where did they come from? There's no encampment or herd in sight. What are they doing here? They could likewise be wondering about me, a middle-aged stranger with a gray haversack, knocking about in the wastes in shorts and sandals, slouch hat pulled low against the sun. The Rest House shimmers in the heat several kilometers down the sandy plain separating Jebel Rumm and its mirror reflection, Umm Ishrin. In the distance a Bedouin woman gestures as she and a child crouch over a small fire. I accept their invitation to share some tea, which the woman pours from a *finjan* (cup or

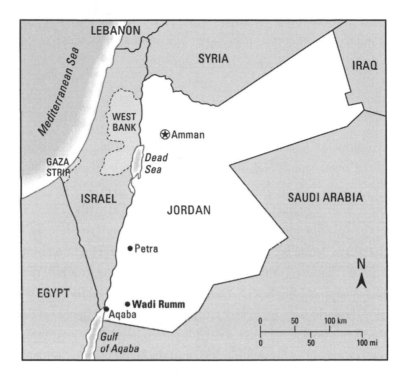

small coffeepot) balanced on crackling twigs. She doesn't bother
to reach for her scarf and veil her face, which is pricked with blue
tattoo marks. Did you see one of our kid goats that strayed from
the flock? she asks me in Arabic. The words shoot out at a clip
I can't follow, and I get her drift more from her gestures. The
young boy runs off to round up a pair of camels at the far end of
the wadi. She points at the tea: *Tfadal, tfadal,* all the while spin-
ning wool on a hand spindle pressed against her thigh as her free
hand unravels the fleece.

Ghor Rumm—Valley of the Moon.

Sundown. A light meal sitting on the empty terrace of one of
the two dusty cafés overlooking the *ghor.* Sudden gust of wind
raises a curtain of sand. Bedouin woman and child, barely visible,
plod through the sandstorm, their flock in wedge formation, toward the village of Rumm, a shantytown of cinderblock and mud

huts and traditional goat-hair tents. In the center of the village is the high-walled Desert Patrol Fort—dating from the Mandate period, or earlier? Fairuz on the radio.

* * *

Dolphins on my mind as I unfurl my sleeping bag in the ruins of the small, square Nabatean temple. Arion, who'd invented the dithyramb, rode to shore on a dolphin's back. He'd been sailing home after winning first prize in a music festival in Sicily. The sailors got greedy, plotted to steal his prize money and have him walk the plank. Arion begged to sing one last song before casting himself into the sea. A dolphin, drawn to the ship by the strains of music, came to Arion's rescue. On my last visit to Nuweiba I'd heard of a Bedouin deaf-mute boy from a small fishing village on the Red Sea who had befriended a wild spotted dolphin. Sometime in the early nineties the dolphin followed the boy's boat to the shore and since then has remained his steadfast friend, swimming with him daily and bringing a steady stream of tourists to the village. Are the sounds that Abdallah emits from his damaged voice box, the crack and frailty of his voice dusted with its own fleetingness, the inverse image of Arion's full-bodied paean to Apollo? Like the thin, piping voice of Kafka's Josephine the Mouse-Singer, "withdrawn and living only in her song."[1]

When I fall asleep the stars are obscured by thin layers of cloud, but later in the night my eyes pop open to a magnificent display aswarm in the heavens. Where would Arion's lyre constellation be? Or am I thinking of Orion the hunter, prized by Dawn and then struck down by Artemis's arrow? Their names, merely the shaping of vowels in the mouth, are almost interchangeable. And what of the fine line drawn in the *tweaking* of their instruments, the one conferring, even enhancing, life, and the other taking it away? "The bow is called Life [*bios*], but its work is death."[2] I'm up in the early hours, scanning the eastern massif before its contours blur in the daylight haze: igneous and dark below, with shale and loose scree rising several meters high against a vertical rock face zebra-striped in earth tones—lighter grays and white toward the top, pocked and creviced and fissured. Bald, flattop (limestone?) summits. Time, which in French also denotes the weather, *le temps*: the fierce winter winds abrading the sandstone while sudden torrential rains turn at the blink of an eye into flash floods that cleave and gouge through the massifs, scooping and plowing a maze of gullies, fanning out into canyons and stepped ravines with ledges and crannies and gashed with cool, dark recesses. Yesterday in Wadi Sid I circled in reverence a pristine pool of rainwater sunk deep into the stone.

Lawrence's Spring. Ain Shellaleh. About an hour's steep hike from the Rest House encampment. This is where Lawrence was struck with wonder at the sight of an old Bedouin swimming naked in a rock pool below the spring.[3] I reach its source somewhat out of breath, following the remains of a Nabatean aqueduct. Fig and date palm—slender, nubile—shoot straight out of the cracked limestone. Wide, irregular patches of mint. Maidenhair. A trickle of water down the rock face glistens in the sun. Lawrence's pool has shrunk to a puddle. A falcon—peregrine?—perched on a boulder swivels its head. An Arabic inscription on the canyon wall above the spring praises Allah.

I'm in what looks like a huge sandstone amphitheater. Sheer, striated walls have a potter's burnished earth tints. The falcon takes flight, gliding on a thermal, its high-pitched call piercing the air. *Kee, kee-a.* Several entablatures are carved into the rock wall near the spring. I could swear I am looking at Hebrew or proto-Hebrew inscriptions, but epigraphists have identified the letters as Nabatean, carved under a niche with two schematic designs, or "eye idols," and identical to the sort of writing found in the canyon leading into Petra. The inscriptions are addressed to al-Uzza, goddess of the evening star, patroness of perennial springs, and to al-Kutba, the scribal god of Gaia:

On a ledge a little way off, to the left of the spring:

I manage a scrambling ascent to the upper level of the canyon high above Lawrence's Spring. Enter a narrow passage leading to, but still a distance from what I imagine to be the twin peaks of Jebel Rumm. Halfway up, just before the crevice becomes too narrow to negotiate: a lovely, solitary tree with a white trunk and lobed leaves, not unlike a young maple. Someone has left a jagged piece of mirror on a small ledge. Voice of the muezzin calling to prayer resounds between the canyon walls. Not so much a voice as a muffled cry carried by the wind, more like a rumble. Tristram grackles dip and glide overhead. I'm alerted to their presence by the familiar (Dead Sea) shrill cry—three notes: short, long, and again short. Amphibrach? Meter in birdsong. Or, as Arabic tradition has it for that matter, the lift and fall of the camel's hoof.

A second falcon dives low over the flinty floor bed, looking for prey to scoop up in its talons.

A last backward glance before heading back to the Nabatean ruins below. After touching base I head south to Abu Aina, a huge upright boulder twice my height scored with Thamudic in-

scriptions and stick figures along with crude zoomorphic forms:
a camel, a long-horned ibex, gazelles. I scribble in my notebook
some of the odder-looking inscriptions:

$$\phi \; \mathfrak{d} | \; \mathfrak{o} \; \mathfrak{d} \mathfrak{C} \mathfrak{d} \; \mathfrak{d} \; \mathfrak{\Leftrightarrow} \mathfrak{\rightarrow} \; \mathfrak{d} \; \mathfrak{l}$$

From here I can see for the first time the bastion-like Jebel
Khazali, Lawrence's "glowing square," and behind its implacable
mass a loose chain of bare, chocolate- and cream-colored mountains, with buttes and undulant dunes receding from view all the
way to the Gulf of Aqaba. Wherever the eye rests, landforms and
outcroppings glow in the sun like crumbling beds of embers.

Imagine reducing the monumental scale of Wadi Rumm to a
personal aesthetic of tonal harmonies—volume, texture, the play
of light—like a Morandi arrangement of ceramic jars, dissolving
the rock face in rapid, loose brushwork.

I sit and write in the shade of an acacia before venturing in the
direction of Jebel Khazali, heading across a wide-open stretch of
ground strewn with small sharp stones that geologists call regs.
There's a Bedouin squatting in the middle of the flatlands. He
doesn't so much as blink when I cross his path. Just keeps sitting on his haunches and looking straight ahead. In the words of
Koheleth, "Better a handful of quietness than both hands full of
labor and striving after the wind."

Skirting a herd of camels, their hind legs hobbled to prevent
them from roaming too far, I can't help smiling to myself as one
of Taha Muhammad Ali's homespun stories comes to mind: the
poet offers a friend of his, a regular visitor to his souvenir shop
in Nazareth, the bribe of a small olivewood camel if he agrees to
listen to his poems. A camel for a poem.[4]

Naqa: the she-camel of pre-Islamic poetry, for so long laden
(in my mind) with symbolic meaning: my reading of Doughty,
Stetkevych, Borges ("In his *mu'allaqa*, Zuhayr says that in the

course of his eighty years of pain and glory many is the time he has seen destiny trample men, like an old blind camel");[5] of Canetti at the camel market (gruesome) in Marrakesh; of the avant-gardist Avot Yeshurun and the recurring, transformative presence of the camel in his poetry ("How the camel always sticks out its neck to see what I'm writing,"[6] he jots down in a note appended to an early sequence of poems); and, more recently, of the remarkable Jerusalem-born Aref el-Aref, who fought alongside the Turks in World War I, was captured by the Russians, escaped, trekked back to Palestine, joined the Arab nationalists, fled the British into the hills of Trans-Jordan (after rumors spread of his orchestrating the Nebi Musa riots of 1920), was pardoned by British High Commissioner Herbert Samuel, and—having accepted a posting as district officer of Beer-sheva—published in Arabic, in 1935, the first ethnographic study of the Bedouin tribes of the Negev, which would be translated into Hebrew the following year and into English in 1944 under the title *Bedouin Love, Law, and Legend: Dealing Exclusively with the Badu of Beersheba*. "To the Badawi," Aref el-Aref writes, "the camel is almost the keystone of his economic life, a source of happiness, yet a symbol of sadness. The camel serves in time of victory, plays a part in defeat, is used for riding and raiding, to carry brides and bridegrooms, the sick and the halt and the blind."[7]

So why refuse to mount one of the high, caparisoned beasts lined up daily in front of the Government Rest House? Why not trot or lope about the sand dunes for an hour or two like other travelers, day-trippers for the most part, on their way to Petra? I can remember being hoisted as a child onto a kneeling camel's back and anticipating the mount's sudden forward jerk as it rose, straightening its hind legs first, to its full height. Sometime in the late fifties or early sixties we'd been invited to share a meal with Bedouin in the Negev. A lamb had been slaughtered and roasted over a bed of embers. Had we driven south of Beer-sheva alone?

Surely some friend of my parents had arranged the encounter—my first—with the Bedouin. I seem too to recall a snapshot taken of me sitting cross-legged in front of the dark entrance of a tent, cradling—could it be!—an old rifle on my knees. But the photograph has long disappeared, lost or misplaced between one way station or another in my own peregrinations, though I can still retrace its contours in my mind—"I pray for your souls, camel and boy, / who set out in innocence and together won't come back."[8]

*   *   *

Morning call of the muezzin, amplified by the Rumm massif: the sounds are rising, it seems, from deep within the range itself and not from the squat bluff minaret in the center of the village. An elaborate, sinuous call that stretches as if to infinity. Returned last night dead tired after a long trek to Khazali—also known as Qasr Ali before the name was elided by Lawrence—and back. I'd crossed the sand plain in the dark, stubbing my toes against rocks and, too tired to rent one of the pup tents behind the Rest House, simply flopped down in the hospitality tent, which that night was fortunately empty. Fell asleep to the sound of young male voices talking and singing late into the night, and the thrumming of an oud.

Yesterday, on my way to Khazali, I'd first crossed over to the tip of Umm Ashrin, "Mother of Twenty." The sun was setting, and its dying rays softened the face of the mountain where dunes swept up to its base like the frozen crest of a wave. I quickened my pace, determined to get there before nightfall. Midway I heard the piping of a flute and, turning, saw advancing toward me a herd of black-haired goats led by a young Bedouin girl riding sidesaddle on a donkey. She wore a blue embroidered dress and a black scarf wound tightly around her head. To my surprise she slid off her donkey, the way a child might swing off a bike before coming to a full stop, called out to me in a husky voice, *mahaba*, and asked where I was from. Al-Quds, Jerusalem, I answered. She had sharp, intelligent features that not unlike the contours and colors of Wadi Rumm seemed at once bold and a touch wistful, even dreamy, like the tune she played on her reed flute. "Indak qalam?" she asked. It took me awhile to grasp what she was saying. "Qalam?" I asked, and she replied, "Naam." It suddenly dawned on me that she was asking for a pen or pencil, which I pulled out of my knapsack and handed to her. She nodded in gratitude, mounted her donkey, and trotted in pursuit of her flock, which was now closing in on a Bedouin encampment where the darkening vertical folds of Khazali soared skyward like organ pipes. "The good walker," writes Segalen, "follows his course without interrogating at each step the sole of his shoe."[9]

Framed on one of the walls of the Rest House is a large topographical map of the region as well as the opening verses of Koran *surāh* 89: *The Dawn*, which refers, apparently, to Wadi Rumm: "Hast thou not seen how thy Lord did with Ad, Iram of the pillars, the like of which was never created in the land, and Thamud, who hollowed the rocks in the valley. . . . Thy Lord unloosed on them a scourge of chastisement; surely thy Lord is ever on the watch."

How is it that Arabic, with all the romantic appeal of its sun and moon letters, remains beyond my ken? My sporadic efforts to learn the language have ended in repeated failures: the molding of its consonants in the mouth and in the very depths of the throat where the Adam's apple bobs, its ingenious root system and internal play of vowels, projected a world of riches even as it receded from view—disarticulated, illusory, like the *naqa* bearing away its litter and swallowed up, so Labid tells us, in the shimmering haze: "How they stirred your passion, the day they climbed / and hid themselves in the curtained howdahs with creaking tents."[10]

From the verandah of the Rest House I watch the morning light feather and stroke and then, with the sun ascendant, dazzle the sandstone pillars of Umm Ishrin. Who is it the Lord is watching in *The Dawn surāh*? They came from the heart of Arabia. They rolled up their belongings and struck camp, herded their livestock with the seasonal rains, and trekked northward in search of pasture. Families banding together into tribes and confederations, dispersing and reassembling, as they drifted from one way station to another, laying claim to the sweet-water wells, or scraping seep holes (*thamail*) in the gravel beds of wadis and setting up their stone idols for a season before moving on, leaving behind the faintest of clues, traces of their encampment "like the tattoo-marks seen on the back of a hand."[11]

Stinkwort. Sun rose. Sweet-smelling lavender cotton. Jericho oxeye. Anabasis. Shrubby sea blite. Wormwood. Tassel hyacinth.

Late morning, heading north along the length of Umm Ashrin with the intention of rounding its spur and returning along its eastern flank. Once again I stop in my tracks, spellbound by four—no, five   haunting notes of the *shababa*, resounding from afar in the stony tract separating the two ranges. A desert riff of leave takings. Prolonged. Reprised. Tidings that bind and loosen the heart. "The poem is lonely. It is lonely and *en route*."[12] After two hours, despairing of ever reaching the tip of the range, I turn into a wide, gravelly wadi that appears to slice through Umm Ashrin. I've convinced myself that by following the dry riverbed I'll eventually exit on the eastern flank of the mountain. A slow, steady ascent, surrounded by gigantic boulders. Swales of sand, which make it difficult to plod forward. I don't seem to be making any headway. Vistas of craters and strange landforms shaped by sandblasting winds. Sheer cliffs drop into twisting parched watercourses braided with alluvial debris from winter torrents. I keep misgauging distances and, with only half a liter of water left, in the end decide to turn back, grateful when I finally reach the shale and flint-bed pavement of the *ghor* with its rose sandbanks and deposits of windblown loess. I am reminded of the opening lines of Yeshurun's poem "Camel and Boy," which I had attempted to translate before leaving for Wadi Rumm: "And the sand is a scroll whose script a foot / well-versed to the scorching sand probes."[13] In Hebrew the verb stem *mashash*—to feel, touch, grope—resonant with the biblical tale of twinship, birthright, and deceit, of hunter and of gatherer: "So Jacob drew close to his father Isaac, who felt him and wondered. 'The voice is the voice of Jacob, yet the hands are the hands of Esau.' "[14]

Pudding stones.

Scorch marks on the plain, the remains of small fires lit by the Bedouin while herding their goats or camels: stones set in a circle and blackened by smoke, a scattering of ashes, charred twigs, fibrous bits of tinder. Although still holding on to nomadic ways, their days of covering vast distances have long ended. The abundance of hidden perennial springs is what brought a handful of Arabian tribes—among them the Thamud and Ad—to Wadi Rumm and Petra (biblical Edom and Moab) in the first place, over two thousand years ago. Petra, with its impregnable walls and inner grounds offering protection from potential foes, would become the focal point of their centrifugal wanderings; eventually, as they developed ingenious ways of trapping and conserving water in subterranean cisterns, they became known as the Nabatu, which medieval Arab lexicographers took to mean "a man digging for water."

There is nonetheless something to be said for throwing yourself on the mercy of a new language. Reduced to a babble of confused tenses, of signs that hoard their meaning, leaving you gasping for words no sooner drilled than forgotten: the simplest sentence yawns open and you stare into *tohu*, the unformed (the *confound-*

ing, if one attends to the Hebrew etymology), like Antara's black steed, whimpering on the point of extinction: "Had he known the art of conversation, he would have protested, / and had he been acquainted with speech, he would have spoken to me."[15] But the genius of language reveals itself precisely when it crumbles in your hands.

In the evening I talk to Hisham, the oud player whose strains I'd heard the previous night. He's recorded the folk music of the local tribes and has been hired by the Rest House to play for the tourists, mostly Europeans, who come in groups and explore the desert safari-style. Yesterday, as I was tramping back from the Khazali, a dozen jeeps raising red billows of dust hurtled past me toward the end of the reg plain in order to catch the sun setting behind Jebel Rumm. I'd witnessed the same scene some years back in the Sahara in Tunisia, not far from the Algerian border. I'd been standing with some Bedouin on the rim of a huge, ribbed sand dune. One of them was gently stroking a young fennec fox tucked under his robe, when a low rumbling sound broke the stillness of the desert. A convoy of jeeps drove into view and stopped at an adjoining dune, where people jumped out and aimed their cameras at the setting sun while engines were revved for the return to a nearby oasis, and the last ray blipped over the horizon.

I ask Hisham if he is familiar with the pre-Islamic poets of the *Mu'allaqat*. Of course, he beams. Imru al-Qays, Tarafa, Zuhayr. Hold on, I tell him, and run to my tent to dig out of my knapsack my copy of Arberry's translation of the seven odes, which I show to Hisham. He recites by heart, half chanting, the opening lines of Labid's *qasida*: "The abodes are desolate, halting-place and encampment too, / at Mina; deserted lies Ghaul, deserted alike Rijam, / and the torrent-beds of Er-Raiyan—naked shows their trace, / rubbed smooth, like letterings long since scored on a stony slab." Hearing the *qasida* recited in the mouth of a Bedouin makes me infinitely happy, and even though I can't understand a word of the original I allow my index finger to skip over the English text like a mad-happy divining rod.

So too, stumbling upon graffiti after graffiti scored into the black varnish of upright stones, boulders, and sheltering rock faces brings to life the little knowledge I had acquired, reading the orientalists, of the thousands of inscriptions, rock drawings, and standing stone idols that crop up in the desert wastes. For the most part, as discussed earlier, these are embryonic texts—genealogies, names, curses, thanksgivings, declarations of love (and, as I had discovered in *Ancient Records from North Arabia*, sexual conquests), warnings, and boasts—written in Nabatean and Thamudic script. The former resembles ancient Hebrew and Aramaic; the latter displays an odd, childlike mixture of geometric forms (bearing an uncanny resemblance to computer-generated dingbats) and near-pictograms, like the inscription I lean down to admire on the foundation wall of the temple of Allat:

Surely this is what Labid saw on one of his journeys to the court of al-Hira in the north, just west of the Euphrates, where tradition has it he made his reputation as a young poet. Traces on stone, a scattered, nomadic writing whose archaic orthography the poet might or might not—since Arabic writing emerged from the chrysalis of the long, hooked Nabatean characters—have been able to decipher. Scant vocables dispersed across the desert's vast theater like the archipelagos of a fractured syntax. By the time Labid and his fellow qasidists came on the scene, the Nabatean kingdom and its lost city carved in the malleable red rock had been extinct for some three hundred years, and the generations that survived the late Roman and Byzantine incursions had reverted to their nomadic origins.

Listening to Hisham's strumming on the oud and to the muezzin's call to prayer, I have begun to think that the acoustic effects of the bare mountains may have had as strong an influence on the Arabian herdsmen's decision to remain in the region as the availability of water. Bewildered by the play of sounds rebounding from the cliffs, they built their sanctuaries where the imposing rock face seemed to speak in its own strange accents, at once human and otherworldly.

"Are there still blackened orts in the stone-waste of Ed-Darráj and el-Mutathallam, mute witnesses to where Umm Aufá once dwelt?"[16]

Atargatis, dolphin goddess, patroness of the forlorn traveler, with a major sanctuary in the seaport of Ashkalon and another on the Euphrates. Lured into the desert by music. According to al-Kindi, taking his cue from the Pythagoreans, each string of the oud stood for a different humor, which in turn corresponded to the four elements: fire, earth, air, and water. The sea's echo in the wilderness. A man digging for water.

What tectonic ripple thrust up this massive agglutination of grains—igneous, metamorphic? Marine sediments: chalk and limestone, chert, shale and marl (the badlands around the Dead Sea) and petrified shells, including the fossil remains of sea urchins where the Tethys Ocean once covered even the summits of the desert.

*   *   *

I follow a goat path to a ledge called, in Arabic, the little slippery place, with a view across the sand stretches and the village of Rumm to the west. Rest in the shade of a boulder before penetrating deeper into the canyon. Large pool of rainwater in another hollow shaped by the winter torrents. A pair of red dragonflies skims and jigs above the water. A young Bedouin boy and girl, barefoot and as nimble as their flock, keep disappearing into the maze of narrow gorges in search of stray kid goats bleating from within the folds of rock. On my return journey I stumble upon petroglyphs incised on a huge boulder halfway down the slope:

At the bottom of the cliff more drawings and Thamudic inscriptions scattered on several waist-high boulders. Ibex, human forms, camels, birds, and what appears to be a man standing (dancing?) on the hump of a camel:

A turquoise lizard pokes its head out of a fissure and sucks in its thimbleful of air.

For desert life, survival is synonymous with the lessons of frugality. The structure of plants, even those growing in the flat, sandy plain, is designed to draw sustenance from the least moisture, and when a shrub dries out (or sheds part of its body to reduce water loss), a Bedouin strips its bark into rope or uses its woolly stems and roots for remedies or for kindling a fire to make his prized *qahweh* (coffee) and to dream by, with one eye on his herd as it crops the ephemeral spring fuzz. Pare away the superfluous, leaving only the indispensable, concentrated and pulped, like the essence distilled from dwarf herbs hidden in crevices.

*   *   *

Return to Abu Aineh to get a better look at the Thamudic inscriptions. Two loose knots of goats, cut off from the rest of the herd, bawl across twin peaks. Once the Nabateans had driven in their stakes for more than a season, it couldn't have taken them long to realize the strategic importance of the region extending from Aqaba to Petra and running straight up to the Hauran, the eastern desert of modern day Syria: they had inadvertently stumbled upon the major caravan trade route between Arabia and the eastern Mediterranean ports—Ashkalon, el-Arish, and Gaza—from which ships loaded with spices and incense sailed westward. At first they applied their nomadic skills as highwaymen, raiding the long lines of caravans emerging from Arabia. "Who is this that cometh out of the wilderness like pillars of smoke, perfumed with myrrh and frankincense, with all powders of the merchant?"[17]

Again the voice of the muezzin reverberating in the mountains behind the Rest House, amplified and converted into a ghostly ensemble of wind instruments. I trudge to the southern tip of the Rumm massif. Crimson sands of the Khazali. Traces of a Nubian site, including the remains of a cistern. Not far off a black wheatear, white-crowned, pecks in the sand then flits away, blending into the shadow of a boulder.

Dun-colored gecko with minute suction cups for toes.

A huge flying buttress with a chunk of sky peering through reminds me of Bialik's "Mete Midbar" (The Dead of the Desert), which was inspired by a tale from the Talmud. A Jew encounters an Arab merchant in the desert and is shown the generation of Israelites who died in the wastes because of their lack of faith. There they lie (ecstatic-looking?), morphed into boulders of all sizes and shapes. One frozen figure has a knee raised in such a manner that the merchant can pass under it astride his camel, his spear held upright. The wilderness of Zin. But the marvel of Bialik's poem is that writing from Odessa in 1902, before having set foot in Palestine, the poet reads the desert like a seasoned nomad.

Written in hexameters, which in itself recalls the long metrical pattern (*tawil*) common to the *qasida*, "The Dead of the Desert" is a poem of primordial awakening, of the emergence of form out of the formless, as the dormant giants, these golem-like figures of rebellion embedded in the geological strata of the desert, are briefly stirred awake and given voice—called to arms?—in the eye of a raging sandstorm. The poem can be read allegorically as the clarion call of the Hebrew renaissance. But its success surely lies in the poet's lexical engagement with the scarred desert terrain—the withering heat and the "warping and weaving"[18] of a circling bird of prey, the play of moonlight on the brow of a rock, the charge of a Bedouin on his horse—which provides the setting for a layered narrative, an account of an account (a Talmudic spin on Numbers 14:26–30), retold by a Bedouin elder—the Other who bears (and lays bare) our own secrets. The dead and their weaponry, stretched out and "hardened forever with blows of the hammer of time," have the look of an ancient script incised on stone, while a speckled asp rearing its body is likened to a column scored with hieroglyphs. Romance of origins, of landforms in violent repose, where words and the arid wilderness share a grammar of rupture (textbook geology: "erosion begets deposition") and rejuvenation.

From a bird's-eye view the topography of Wadi Rumm might be compared to an hourglass, with the gravel plain—the Valley of the Moon—serving as the long, narrow passageway or neck between the outlying mountains and the curved bulbs of their sand deposits:

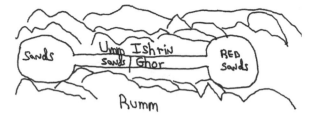

Around noon I reach the narrow canyon slicing through the bulk of Khazali after first walking along its west façade to admire in the distance the broken corona of buttes emerging from the sand's crimson billows—migrating dunes—stretching south, toward Arabia.

Ed-Darráj: the way, route, course, flight of steps . . .

In broad daylight I can see numerous stick figures incised high on the walls of the narrow gorge leading into the Khazali, including what appears to be a female figure giving birth:

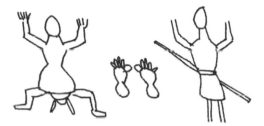

More drawings of ibex. Human figures in pairs, some with arms raised (thumbs up), others lowered (thumbs down):

While I'm resting in the shade of a thorn tree, a sparrow-size bird with a brown rump and rose-red feathers alights near me and with several short hops, accompanied by sweet chirping notes, practically brushes against one of my outstretched legs.

For the Nabateans, what may have started off as a "life of brig-andage,"[19] in the words of Diodorus, eventually turned into a highly efficient caravan service from Arabia, India, and East Africa to Petra, and from there across the Negev to the Mediterranean. They consolidated their tribes into a kingdom with city-cum-trading-posts in northern Arabia (Medain Saleh, where Doughty saw scratched on rock in 1876 their "strange, crawling letters"[20]), in the Negev (Avdat, Nitzana, Shivta), and along the Jordanian highlands (Kirbet Tannur) high above the Syrian-African rift, leading to Palmyra. Petra would become their prodigious fortress-capital ringed by "purple gloom of cliffs,"[21] and it is undoubtedly in Petra that the Nabateans transformed themselves, over several generations, from nomadic herdsmen to city dwellers with a taste for the good life: "The king holds many drinking-bouts in mag-nificent style, but no one drinks more than eleven cupfuls, each time using a different golden cup."[22]

Pulse of the desert in the brainpan.

I strike up a conversation with Mahmoud, a tour guide from Petra who has parked his jeep nearby. He's here with an American couple—the man, it turns out, is originally from Israel. Studied agriculture in Rehovot, but now runs a bakery with his wife in Santa Barbara. Mahmoud has arranged for them to share a tent for the next five days with local Bedouin camped behind the Khazali. He writes on an envelope the names of some of the low shrubs growing in the area: *rathem, ratha, ajram.*

By the time Antara came along, the *qasida* was bound by an oral tradition as tenacious as the gray-leaved sagebrush. A poet knew what had to be done. How to go through the poem's paces. Remembrance (of a lost love). Journey. Boast. But what comes next, the variations on familiar themes, the attention to detail—who was it who spoke (scornfully) of the *qasida*'s "atomism"?—the swerves and curvets in loquaciousness take your breath away, like the first flush of spring in the desert tracts. To write along the seam—the fault line—"betwixt the world destroyed and world restored."[23]

Al-Uzza, "The Powerful One," appears in a bilingual inscription from the island of Cos: "To the goddess al-Uzza," reads the Nabatean dedication; and in Greek "To the goddess Aphrodite." The blending, amalgamating of names and tongues, and don't forget Eros, "who loosens the limbs"—Aphrodite's faithful attendant, the child of Poverty and Resource, spotted on more than one occasion riding a dolphin.

A life-size statue of Aphrodite-Venus, attended by winged Eros straddling a dolphin, was uncovered in the ruins of the bathhouse of Roman Bet Shean. Carved in marble from Aphrodisias, the trio must have been lashed to the deck of a ship plying between the coast of Asia Minor and the Levant before being trundled across the Jezreel valley that slopes eastward toward the dry, bottomed-out Jordan Rift. Bet Shean couldn't have been more than two days' journey by camel from Wadi Rumm. The traveler would have circumvented the salt swamps and cracked badlands of the Dead Sea, bivouacked for the night, perhaps, in the oasis town of Jericho, and then completed the final stretch of his journey the next morning, riding along the gnawed margins of the Jordan River that meanders sluggishly over the entire width of the great Rift valley flanked by bare, marl hills. Approaching Nyssa-Scythopolis as the sun withdrew behind the sharp fault scarps to the west.

Aphrodite leans slightly forward, her left knee absorbing the weight of her body. The gazing eye completes the gentle tilt of her absent head. Her hands are missing as well, but the angle of her right arm suggests that she is reaching to cover her breast, while her left arm slants toward her private parts. Venus Pudica. Eros and the dolphin ride the crest of a wave grazing the calf of her leg. Eros is a touch pensive for someone on a joyride, though his lips arch into the sliver of a smile that chimes with and replicates in miniature the faint curvature of Aphrodite's torso.

It is Diotima who speaks of Eros as the offspring of Poverty and Resource. Hence, she asserts, desire, suspended between extremes, expressing at once a need, a necessary lack, and a stratagem or craft, is neither wise nor ignorant, but rather dangles somewhere in between, embracing its own passage or transit—its own liminality. Eros in the guise of a daimon-like man, neither god nor mortal, riding the inward curve, the wavelike trough of an echo.

So Eros the trickster (I seem to recall a glint in the eye of the Bet Shean cupid) lives in abject poverty, even as he schemes after the beautiful and the good; and whatever he gets from his father's side (Resource), Diotima is quick to add, is always slipping away from him—which might well sum up the predicament of many a poet, and reminds me of Imru al-Qays's own confession as he wanders through the Arabian desert: "And I've trekked across many a wadi / bare as the belly of a wild ass, where the lean wolf howls / like an outcast grubbing for scraps."[24] Also coming to mind is Shanfara, the wily brigand-poet, who goes one step further in allying himself with the wolf:

He sets out at dawn, hungry,
    quick into the wind,
slicing down where the ravine ends
    and veering.

        He moves on in pursuit of food.
    it eludes him.
        He howls. His mates respond,
    hunger-worn,

thin as the moon,
    ashen-faced, like arrow shafts
rattling around
    in the hand of a gambler.[25]

Could the anonymous tenth-century anthologizer of the *Book of Strangers* have ridden through Wadi Rumm, copying off boulders and rocks, shrine and *khān* (rest house), the graffiti that gave vent, for the most part, to the traveler's homesickness as he trekked through the desert? He does mention sojourning in al-Ramla (Palestine) and even quotes a translated inscription from the *hijr* (rocky country) of Thamud, most likely Madain Salih.[26] As a latecomer, would he have been able to read these quixotic signs, suggestive of a host of Semitic languages?

Echolocation, also known as dolphin sonar.

Amassing material goods, the Nabateans turned Petra into a showcase of Greco-Roman funerary architecture, monumentally carved into the soft Nubian sandstone. On the surface, at least, it appears that an austere, nomadic culture, which initially refused to till the soil, abstained from drinking wine, and worshipped the blank face of stones, had become Hellenized: they expanded their pantheon of gods; developed a centralized, royal court; produced figurative art—framed by elaborate grape and vine ornamentations—and pottery of great delicacy; engaged, intensely, ingeniously, in agriculture; and even dwelled in square stone homes. Given all this, the Dolphin Goddess could possibly represent the long arm of their commercial ambitions, for the passage across the Mediterranean was the last stage in the transit of exotic goods that passed through their hands. But from the stelae carved into the rock face at Lawrence's Spring, and from the many near-identical niches containing schematically carved "eye idols" and blank faces in the defile snaking into Petra, it seems the Nabateans did not completely abandon the worship of their old desert gods, such as Allat, Dusares, al-Uzza, and al-Kutba. Might there have been two rival aesthetic and ideological viewpoints contending for popular appeal—one Hellenic, syncretic, figurative, and the other cultic, exclusive, iconoclastic, rooted in its nomadic past and nourished by the luminous void of the Empty Quarter in Arabia's heartland, through which the Nabateans threaded on camels freighted with merchandise?

Commenting on the Song of Songs, the author of the Zohar writes: "Out of the wilderness [*midbar*], that is, 'from one who speaks [*meddaber*].' "[27]

The Nabatean kingdom would eventually disintegrate, mainly because of changing trade routes and the annexation of the monarchy by Rome. But the Koran ascribes the decline—or rather the destruction—of the Ad and Thamud tribes to arrogance and greed. The sinister, moral tale appears in several *surāh*s and involves a she-camel as a Sign. The prophet Salih is sent to reprimand the tribes, victims of a severe drought, for their waywardness. The privileged classes have been preventing the poor from bringing their livestock to the few remaining springs and wells. Salih puts the tribesmen to the test by letting loose into their territory an undernourished *naqa*. Instead of feeding the she-camel—"to her a draught and to you a draught"[28]—the Thamud slaughter the beast and hoard the meat, and Allah in retribution wreaks havoc on the Thamud.

But what to make of the seemingly haphazard dispersion of pictographs in the desert wastes? Do these stick figures of hunting scenes and human prowess have a purely mimetic function, or might they not be transformative, endowed with meaning and an aura we can no longer decipher or experience since we have long ceased to be desert dwellers? Certainly the figure careening on the hump of a camel, or the woman with a child crowning from between her legs, or the outline of a pair of feet, suggests a wider, more arcane context. And what if the specific sites, the countless boulders and weathered rocks and overhangs on which the glyphs are incised, were somehow connected to one another and resembled minuscule relay stations, foci of energy, invisible pressure points in what was once a sacred enclosure? "Curb your heart from speculating and your mouth from speaking," warns the

Book of Creation, "and if your heart races ahead, turn back. For this reason it is said, 'and the creatures surged forward and returned.' So a pact was drawn."[29]

Emitting clicks and whistles, a dolphin creates for itself an "acoustical picture" as ultrasounds roll back from shadow objects in its aqueous world.

A blistered toe has me hobbling back to the Rest House, and *pace* Segalen, I find myself constantly interrogating the sole of my shoe—well, sandal. How often has the nearly intelligible been equated with the exotic? The self-effacing sign that lures even as it denies access, and proceeds to cover its tracks: "Out I brought her," boasts Imru al-Qays, "and as she stepped she trailed behind us / to cover our footprints the skirt of an embroidered gown."[30] So there you have it, charged speech and the needlepoint of its own evanescence embellishing the margins of our lives. Traces, in Arabic *rusum*, on which the edifice of pre-Islamic desert poetry is built. What was it Noah Stern had written, upon spying a Bedouin woman on the outskirts of Jericho? "A faint sign in the sand / the daywake leaves, gathered into the past."[31]

And *dhikr*, remembrance (of the beloved), which in time will turn into a fundamental tenet of devotion in Islam. I wish I could call to mind my first lip-biting efforts at decoding words on the page as a child. *See Jane Run.* For it seems, as the years accelerate, that I have been returning to and reliving, in an ever-tightening circle, a form of unknowing, of speechless awe. Was I tracing, even here, in this stony tract, the unbridgeable gap felt as a child (for I had been a slow, recalcitrant learner) between words and objects? The aporia of reading, in the sense of being at a loss, of having, as the Greek suggests, "no way out." And now, puzzling over so many curious signs carved into stone, I can't help feeling that Wadi Rumm has become my own open-air school where I stride out daily, stumbling upon cryptic lines scrawled in a generous hand on the broad face of the desert.

When I ask Mahmoud the name of the bird I'd seen earlier, he chuckles and explains that it was a common sparrow whose feathers were dusted red from perching on the ledges and nooks of Nubian sandstone.

Dark, raised brows of the low-slung Bedouin tents.

Galilean Centos

If one bathe in them three days . . . he will, by the grace
of God, be healed of any scab, swelling, fistula or other
ailment with which he may be afflicted.

Al-Muqaddasi

Fathi is at the wheel while his son dozes slumped in the backseat
as we head for the thermal springs of el-Hammeh.
　Mu'awiya hasn't had much sleep. He's spent the night in Abu
Hikmat's tent, rigged up for the summer at the center of a vast
plain the locals call Marj Battuf—the Flooded Valley—which extends for miles between two low mountain ranges. The land has
been cultivated for hundreds of years by half a dozen Arab villages, including Sakhnin, hugging the lower slopes on the other
side of the mountain at the northern end of the plain. Soon after I'd
moved in with the Halilehs, Fathi had suggested we drive over to
his field in the late afternoon. We had cut through Sakhnin, heading east to the neighboring village of Arabeh, and then chugged up
the mountain before winding down into Marj Battuf. He wanted
to show me his field where he grew tomatoes, squash, green peppers, and the popular *faqqus*—a long, thin cucumber—as well as
okra and melon. We had filled two bags with okra that his wife,

Radda, would cook for dinner. Bending over a waist-high golden thistle, Fathi had run his hand down the stem, removing the spiny leaves in one quick stroke: "Here, eat this," and he bit into his half of the stem. It tasted like celery, only sweeter and less crunchy. But I was soon to discover that everything growing in Marj Battuf partook of a distinct savor and aroma, which had to do—so Fathi explained to me—with the annual flooding of the plain by winter rains, causing the red topsoil and its yield of sunflowers and wheat and barley to remain saturated well into the hot summer months, while the light breeze blowing in from the Mediterranean soothed the plain toward evening and brought the villagers in droves to their fields to pick the crops or simply to sit under their makeshift shelters and talk softly into the encroaching dark.

Mu'awiya had spent the night in Abu Hikmat's tent in order to sprinkle a sulfur compound on their rows of tomatoes in the morning. The job had to be done at sunrise, when the tomatoes were still drenched in dew, and the white, powdery pesticide would stick to their surface. Abu Hikmat, now in his seventies, widowed and recently remarried, was a die-hard traditionalist. While most of the villagers and townsfolk rolled up their mattresses and drove back home after a light supper under the stars, he set up sleeping quarters in his fields for the entire summer, just as in the old days when, at the end of the wheat harvest, practically every stubble field boasted its roomy family tent and Marj Battuf buzzed with life.

After taking care of his father's tomatoes, Mu'awiya had clambered into the grain-filled wagon hitched to Abu Hikmat's old Massey Ferguson tractor for the ride back to Arabeh, where the wheat would be poured into a huge, rusty contraption that creaked and rattled and spat out the winnowed seeds into a row of burlap sacks. By 8 a.m., when we arrived to pick him up, nearly a hundred sacks were piled beside the barn. Two went into the trunk of Fathi's Subaru, recompense for Mu'awiya's assistance. Though

I suspect there was more behind the transaction, such as the box of Viagra I saw Fathi slip into Abu Hikmat's hand—prescribed, Fathi later informed me, at his request from his own doctor as a favor to his friend, who was too proud to approach his own physician.

Leaving Arabeh, I crank the window down as we speed along due east. Fathi announces a pit stop and swerves into what looks like a single-pump gas station. The owner emerging from a grimy shack is a friend of his, maybe a distant relative (the Halileh clan make up half of Sakhnin). Fathi asks if we can store the two burlap sacks behind his station for the day to ease the weight in the trunk.

We're back on the road, Mu'awiya still fast asleep.

Fathi launches into an animated frame-by-frame account of Saladin's victory over the Crusaders at the Battle of Hittin as we approach the Golani junction. Three years ago he decided to leave his teaching job in Sakhnin and enroll in a yearlong training course for tour guides run by the Society for the Protection of Nature. As a freelance guide, he now works mostly with Arab schools in the Galilee, taking classes out for their annual field trip. But now and then he guides groups of Israeli Jews—when I first arrived in Sakhnin he'd spent the day with doctors and nurses from a hospital in Haifa—and has proved to be a great success. One can easily see why: he knows his history—biblical, Byzantine, Muslim, modern—and his delivery in Hebrew, peppered with native folklore and the occasional risqué joke, is inimitable. He is an enthusiast. The words fly out of his mouth confidently, colorfully. In full swing he has Saladin "rattling the nerves" of the Franks as we cross the junction, and he suddenly asks me, "Do you know why it's called the Golani junction?" Something to do with Israeli troops and the Yom Kippur War, I offer, but no, that's not it at all. You have to go back to '48, he explains. "This is where the first commander of the Golani brigade, named Golan, was ambushed and killed by a small band of Palestinian militia from Tiberius." I turn around in my seat, as if I might catch the ghost of the unfortunate combatant waving feebly from the dusty intersection.

It turns out the ambush had been commandeered by Fathi's uncle, Subhi Shahin. We're descending to the southern tip of the Sea of Galilee as Fathi recounts how his mother's brother had made a name for himself in Tabariyeh as a bandit before joining the Palestinian irregulars on the eve of the Arab-Israeli War of 1948. A wanted man after gunning down Golan, he eventually fled to Syria, joined the PLO, slipped into Jordan, was involved in the attempted assassination of the king, fled back to Damascus, and finally settled in Amman, where he became a successful contractor after being officially pardoned by the Hashemite king. "And what about your mother?" I ask. "Arabs and Jews lived in peace in Tabariyeh until the war broke out and the Haganah attacked the Old City. I'm not saying that the Arab Liberation League didn't put up a fight—the militia here was especially tough. But after the Haganah fired mortars into the city, people started fleeing for their lives, and at some point the British came along with buses and trucks and escorted the remaining Arabs out of the city, some heading for Nazareth, others for Transjordan. My mother and two of her younger brothers ended up in Nazareth. Subsequently she married my father, who lived in Sakhnin, but we've got a lot of relatives in Jordan. Only the poor ones ever bother to contact us." Fathi lets out a quick succession of high-pitched chortles.

Already we're driving alongside the southern tip of the Sea of Galilee, the flat expanse of the Jordan Valley Rift on our right, hot air streaming into the car. It can't be more than ten minutes before we wind up the bare gorge dividing the Golan and Gilead Mountains. I crane my head out the window, trying to catch sight of the Yarmuk flowing into the Jordan, but all I can see are basalt boulders and scorched brush. The ascent soon levels off, and we plunge down to el-Hammeh—Hamat Gader, in Hebrew—where the gorge widens into a broad plain.

Back in May 2000 I had gazed down at the hot springs from the heights of Umm Qais in Jordan. The village was built on top of and around the Greco-Roman site of Gadara, where I'd wandered for several days. For the most part I had the place all to myself, its ruins extending in all directions along the mountain ridge with its panoramic views of the Sea of Galilee, the Golan Heights, and, further north, snow-capped Mount Hermon. But I soon found myself returning to an olive grove pitted with burial tombs on the western margins of Gadara. Sitting in the shade, I had watched the hoopoes pecking for worms and read from my copy of Meleager, born in Gadara in the second century BC. "Tyre of the godlike boys and Gadara's holy earth made him a man," the poet writes in his epitaph. "Lovely Cos of the Meropes looked after the old man in his age. So if you are a Syrian, Salaam! If you are a Phoenician, Naidios! If you are a Greek, Chairè!—And say the same [to me]."[1]

Meleager lived during the drawn-out afterglow of the Alexandrian age. Greek culture had spread from the mainland and Asia Minor to the islands and further east into the heartland of the Levant, where the pan-Hellenes in turn would become, in the poet George Seferis's words, "half-Asiatic." This was a time when the Homeric epic had long given way to the idyll and the lyric, and the latter genre to the even shorter epigram—from the Greek meaning "to mark on the surface, inscribe." What suffered inscription at first were wayside tombs on which the passerby was enjoined to reflect on life's brevity and remember the tomb's occupant. Its lapidary form encouraged a language of greater intimacy, as one voice addressed another across an invisible divide. By the third century BC the chiseled line was largely replaced by ink on parchment, while the amphitheater and choral performance of verse found its rival in the banquet hall, where the writing and reading of epigrammatic poetry became a form of after-dinner entertainment, broadening to include the wine song and the pastoral sketch, and exploring such themes as friendship and—taking its cue from Sappho and Asklepiades, whose verse must have glowed with an antique luster by then—erotic love. Meleager excelled at the last, though what took my breath away were eight lines which could have been written in the same grove where I had jotted down: "flock of sheep in the OG [olive grove]—where the Roman road to Tiberius once cut—lying at noon in a perfect circle in the shade of an old olive tree, like spokes of a wheel. Cicadas working overtime." Here is Meleager in Peter Jay's rendering:

> Noisy cricket, drunk with dew-drops, you sing your country song which fills lonely places with chatter; with sawlike legs and negro [or sunburnt] skin, sitting on the tips of leaves you shriek lyre-music. But dear [friend], utter some new ditty for the woodland nymphs, strike up a tune in response to Pan, so that escaping from Eros I may snatch a midday sleep, lying here beneath a shady plane-tree.[2]

We park under a tall ficus tree and enter the grounds of el-Hammeh, with Mu'awiya, reinvigorated and smiling, running ahead of us. It turns out that Fathi has also visited Umm Qais, which we can just see shimmering in the noon haze to the south and several hundred meters above us, a straggle of squat stone homes dotting its slopes. It makes perfect sense that this had been the location of the Gospel parable of the demonized herd of swine rushing headlong into the Sea of Galilee. Fathi, however, suggests another ancient site—Gergesa—located on a ridge further north, where the bewildered swine would have had less ground to cover before taking the cold plunge into the lake.

It turns out that the thermal springs welling up from the bowels of the earth cover only a fraction of the grounds, which in recent years have been made into a recreation park. As we follow a sign-post to the Central Bath Complex we pass other signs for a Spa Village Hotel, a Sports Ground, a Mini Wildlife Preserve, and even a Crocodile Farm. No wonder Mu'awiya is beaming.

An elevator takes us one floor down to the baths, a complex of large, clover-shaped pools connected by a footbridge and sheltered from the sun by a pagoda-style trellis roof. Mu'awiya is waist-deep in the water, waving to us: "Ta'alu, ta'alu!" (Come!) Beads of water gleam on his chest and the top of his shaved head. Until recently he had a thick crop of dark hair that he would fashion into spikes every morning while his classmates patiently waited outside on their way to school. But just the other day, when I returned from Jerusalem and dropped my knapsack on the picnic table under the grapevine, I'd bumped into the new Mu'awiya as he popped out of the animal enclosure where he'd been feeding his kid goats. "Nice," I said. Of the four Halileh children, Mu'awiya is the youngest. His older brother, Hammudi, had volunteered to crop his hair ("It's a great feeling," he promised, running his hand over the polished top of his own head). Taciturn and athletic, Hammudi works as a stonemason. Then there is spirited, beautiful Asala, in her early twenties, studying draftsmanship at the community college in Sakhnin and about to get married. Sixteen-year-old Mithal, the "brainy one," has finally persuaded her father to let her take a summer job working on an assembly line in Bet Shean in the Jordan Valley.

Fathi eases his back against the poolside as jets of water needle his body. I slip into the steaming water and slowly breaststroke over to him. The pools, giving off a distinct odor of sulfur, are empty except for some elderly, slow-treading pensioners. Nearby, half a dozen extended families—Russian and Arab for the most part—have gathered in animated groups, and a few young couples are sunning on deck chairs.

Ancient Gadara must have extended down to the thermal springs, as it couldn't have been more than a morning's walk before one reached the upper springs, now in Jordan. Meleager writes with felicity of the blooming "mountain-rambling lilies," *thalay d' ouresifoita krina,* which I can easily imagine brushing the knees of those who scrambled down the sloping hills for their daily bath cure. *Ouresifoita* perfectly conveys at once the illusion of mobility at the sight of a scatter of spring blossoms on a mountain (*ouresi*), and their maddening, intoxicating effect, as the Greek *foita* strongly implies. In *Antigone* Eros sets out determinedly: "you who spend the night upon the soft cheeks of a girl, and travel [*foitais*] over the sea and through the huts of dwellers in the wild." Surely Meleager the highlander—who was never short of similes for describing erotic longing—must have had this meaning in mind when he coined the compound. The poem's concluding lines make this poignantly clear: "Meadows, why are you foolishly laughing, bright in your foliage [tresses]? That girl is better than sweet-smelling garlands."[3]

Fathi is amused by my description of the poet: we're both having our backs massaged hydraulically as I ramble on about Meleager, whom I portray as a lady's man and, if we can believe the poetry, a man's man as well—not unlike, I add, the Arab poets of al-Andalus. Yesterday we had listened to a tape of Andalusian lyrics sung by Fairuz, all the while negotiating the gouged dirt road that meanders between the fields of Marj Battuf. Her songs, he had remarked in Hebrew, were "mixed," or "diluted," in his heart. I remember being struck by his choice of words: one speaks in Hebrew of wine being mixed—*mahool*—with water. Fathi is a sizeable man: large forearms, a bulging girth, full lips, and a high, sloping forehead. But when he'd uttered the word *mahool* he had seemed for a moment as light as a rolling ball of tumbleweed. The car had bumped and swerved as Fathi sang along with Fairuz: "A sword cuts when removed from its scabbard, but your eyes cut even when sheathed."

Having tried out the bubble pools and a miniature waterfall, Fathi and Mu'awiya soon join me for an idle half hour in deck chairs, staring at the bathers, reading. Fathi fetches from his knapsack a thin paperback of popular sayings. He likes to collect anecdotes and popular proverbs, he explains, to spice up his guided tours. For example, an equivalent of the English "Don't count your chickens before they're hatched": "Don't say *ful* [broad bean] before you fill the sacks." But *ful* reminds me of my first day at the Halilehs. I'd gone out late in the afternoon for a stroll in Sakhnin, and stopping at an eatery flanked by furniture outlets and window displays of bridal dresses, I had ordered a plate of *ful*. That evening, sitting under the Halileh grapevine I'd told Fathi of my early supper at Mat'am Ibrahim. Fathi guffawed in delight. "You had *ful* for supper!" he said. "We have a saying: '*Ful* is a prince's breakfast, a poor man's lunch, and a donkey's supper.'" Rada had joined us at the table, and hearing of the episode, she let out an emphatic *ah*, smiling as she adjusted her headscarf and repeated the adage.

Fathi flips through the pages of his book and comes up with another saying: "Learning for a child is like striking (chiseling) in stone—*darab hyar*—whereas for an adult," Fathi grins, "it's like striking a donkey—*darab hmar*." There is of course no lack of donkey jokes and sayings in Arabic. Mu'awiya, his ear half-cocked to our conversation, pitches in: "Whoever hoisted the donkey onto the roof will have to bring him down." In another version, Fathi adds, the poor creature finds itself stuck atop a minaret.

It's time to share the cantaloupe Mu'awiya has been lugging in his knapsack. We leave the bath complex for a shaded grove with picnic tables. A middle-aged couple further up the sloping grove nod to us, the man with a mobile phone clipped to his belt, his wife in the traditional *hijab* and a drab gray overgarment reaching down to her ankles. It turns out they're from Baqa el-Gharbiyyeh, a town divided into two, with its eastern neighborhoods lying across the Green Line, in the West Bank. Fathi explains to the man how to get to the thermal springs, but the couple remain fixed to the spot, gazing demurely into space.

I suggest we follow the signs to the ruins of the Roman Baths. Fathi and his son, however, decide to head back to the spa and cool off.

The baths are located directly behind a white-brick mosque in disrepair. Might it have been built by Suleiman Nassif Bey, who during the British Mandate period first dreamed up (and financed) the project of turning the mineral springs into a health resort? His name crops up in an archeological survey of el-Hammeh in the *Journal of the Palestine Oriental Society* (1935), where he is thanked for lodging a team of Hebrew University archeologists headed by E. L. Sukenik. Sukenik had examined the Roman Thermae as well as the amphitheater, even though the true objective of his survey was to uncover the remains of a Byzantine synagogue and its splendid mosaic floor, several hundred meters northwest of the bathhouse. It is for the baths and specifically their Hall of Inscriptions that I have brought Fathi and his son to el-Hammeh. I climb over the barrier marked by a No Trespassing sign and drop into the grounds of the Roman site, asking myself why it has taken me so long to make this visit.

*   *   *

Six years have passed since I visited Gadara and stared down from the heights of Umm Qais at leafy el-Hammeh wedged between two mountain ranges. I'd read Meleager and his near contemporary Philodemos—also a native of Gadara, who eventually drifted to Italy; and I'd dug up whatever I could find on Menippus the Cynic, who preceded Meleager by a century and may have set the tone for all future Gadarene writers, but whose own texts are lost, unless one accepts Lucian's "Dialogues of the Dead" as a translation of Menippus. Diogenes Laertius informs us Menippus was born a slave, and adds to his biographical sketch the following *jeu d'esprit*:

Phoenician by birth, but a Cretan dog:
a Money-Lender-By-The-Day—so he was nicknamed—
    maybe you know Menippus.
At Thebes when his house was burgled
and he lost everything, not understanding what it meant to be a
    Cynic
he hanged himself.[4]

A Cynic was, as the Greek will have it, a dog, and Diogenes of Sinope on the Black Sea, the arch-Cynic, was certainly proud of the comparison. Being a Cynic was synonymous with what would now be called rugged or backwoods individualism. Diogenes himself famously slept in a tub; he was, in Guy Davenport's words, the Athenian Thoreau:[5] his antics and shock tactics—"Plato had defined Man as an animal, biped and featherless, and was applauded Diogenes plucked a fowl and brought it into the lecture-room with the words, 'Here is Plato's Man' "[6]—were designed primarily to expose the fraudulent ways of his times. He was a "Socrates gone mad."[7] He proposed to "debase the coinage"[8] of every custom and convention, and advocated leading a life of utmost simplicity, of self-sufficiency and frankness (*parrhesia*), wherein essential truths might be revealed to the self.

Diogenes lived in the fourth century BC, but his teachings caught on much later, becoming popular particularly during the Greco-Roman period, when the centrality of Athens as a city-state yielded to Panhellenism and the rising influence of provincial

Greek towns in the hinterland. The prevalence in the region of self-styled Cynics—and, for that matter, of a slew of philosophical sects: Epicureans, Sophists, Stoics, Skeptics, Neoplatonists, Peripatetics, Pythagoreans—was, at least in part, a product of the mixing of populations and the infusion of new currents of thought in the wake of Alexander's conquests and the colonization of the East, which had always served as a testing ground for a variety of heterodoxies. All the above-mentioned schools espoused an inward-turning independence of mind, indeed a cosmopolitanism (Diogenes: "I am a citizen of the world") and a debunking of authority that attests to the general flux in which Greek culture found itself as Rome gained ascendancy (in Meleager's time, Gadara was technically a Roman province).

I try to picture ancient Gadara and its environs as yet another breeding place for a type of Levantine Cynic. Gadara with its lovely colonnaded courtyard and half-excavated north theater. One afternoon I'd watched a team of hired hands use grub hoes to laboriously clear the soil from the mouths of the theater's upper entrance gates, from which patrons had once emerged into the sun's glare to find their seats. I'd then strolled over to the smaller west theater, its dark basalt facing the Jordan Valley Rift. Might this stage have been used for the New Comedy and Mime that had spread across the Mediterranean world?

Not far off were the remains of the sacred pool dedicated to the water goddesses and presided over by a marble statuette of Artemis of Ephesus. My favorite statue, however—housed in the local museum, formerly the Ottoman governor's residence—had been that of a (headless) peasant boy bearing fruits in the folds of his uplifted tunic. As I remember, his torso and legs bespoke the earthiness and robustness of a youth native to the land, while the polished marble of his arms, half-raised in a ghostly ellipse, appeared to be bearing the very fruits of Hellenism, admittedly a term as elusive as it is suggestive of light and grace and the divine logos.[9]

The poised figure I'd admired six years ago comes to life in my mind as Fathi's fourteen-year-old son, whom I first met some two weeks ago. Astride a low-slung bicycle, he was maneuvering in tight circles opposite the driveway facing the emerald dome of the mosque of Sakhnin, Masjid Salem. No sooner had I asked him if he knew Fathi than I realized he'd been sent out to scout for me—the Yahud, the Jew who had phoned the previous night. "He's my father," Mu'awiya said, before pedaling vigorously up the driveway of his home.

Would the boy on whom the statue was modeled have spoken Syriac, or perhaps Aramaic? Might he have been bilingual, with a smattering of demotic Greek? Then again the boy might have been a Hellenized Jew from the Galilee, or a Samaritan, or even a Nabatean nomad living on the fringes of Gadara, where he would come to sell the produce of his family's acreage. Of the last possibility Diodorus writes: "There are also other tribes of Arabs, of whom some even cultivate the soil, intermingled with the tax-paying peoples, and (who) share the customs of the Syrians, except that they dwell in tents."[10]

It would take the touch of the best of artisans to incarnate the Hellenized dream of youth—of Meleager's winged Eros—in the figure of the peasant boy rooted to the hills and wadis of biblical Gilead, where Elijah had roamed and where Absalom had hung by his long hair in its dense woodlands. "I've handled a lot of stone in my time," says the sculptor of Tyana, in Cavafy's poem. "But here's my favorite work, created with the most care and feeling. This one—it was a hot summer day and my mind rose to ideal things—this one came to me in a vision, this young Hermes."[11]

I stroll under a high Roman archway fronting the bathhouse and squint up at the meander running along its curve. The arch does not appear in James Silk Buckingham's romanticized sketch of the Roman baths from his visit to the site in 1816, but that may be because the edifice is depicted from afar:

Had the second and third floors of the baths apparent in Buckingham's sketch been destroyed in the devastating earthquake of 1837? The arch or "colonnade screen" is, however, mentioned as having been restored in the preliminary report of three seasons of excavations carried out by a team of Israeli archeologists between 1979 and 1980. It features a lovely meander interlaced with floral patterns, as if it were indeed a river winding through a field of wildflowers. Perhaps the stonemason had in mind the sharp river bends of the Jordan on its journey of twists and turns. It was a "never-ending series of serpentine curves," writes American Lieutenant William Francis Lynch, who daringly coursed down the river in 1848.[12]

Why is it that whenever we step into the ruins of an ancient site our eyes immediately seek out ephemera peeking out from the broken columns and crumbling masonry? I pull out my field guide and pick my way between thorn bushes and fragments of basalt and rubble toward the Roman baths. The grounds are covered in

tall, milky thistle and low-lying Syrian eryngo, the latter display-
ing a bluish tracery of branching stems and thin prickly leaves.
Further along, near the entrance to the Hall of Inscriptions, I catch
sight of the trumpet flower of the bugloss; its color changes while
blooming from red to blue and violet, and it is called in Arabic
henna el-dabeah, henna of the hyena.

This last bit of information I'd picked up a few days ago from
Fathi as we explored the lower slopes of Khirbet Cana, which rises
behind his vegetable field like the gigantic hump of a camel. We
had planned to hike to the top. An archeologist from Seattle and a
handful of American volunteers were clearing what was believed
to be the historical site of the miraculous turning of water into wine
by Jesus at the wedding feast of Cana. As Fathi explained, the Arab
village commonly referred to as Kufr Qana, just north of Nazareth,
was founded at a later date, probably in the wake of a natural disas-
ter or civil strife, which had compelled the inhabitants of Khirbet
Cana to relocate. We were both wearing sandals, making it difficult
to negotiate the thorny burnet that covered the slope, and had to
clamber back down. Standing in the shade of a young pistachio tree
that sprang straight out of an ancient burial cave, Fathi had pointed
to the purple and violet streaks running up the nerves of the bugloss's corolla and pronounced its Hebrew and Arabic names.

Hyenas are rarely seen or heard in the Galilee nowadays, but
they were once very much part of the landscape. There are countless, often blood-chilling Palestinian folktales about the exploits
of the wild, nocturnal creature — the psychological counterpart
and demonic antithesis of the domesticated, all-suffering, dim-
witted yet faithful *hmar*, or beast of burden. Tradition has it that
the hyena lured its human prey to its cave by opening its mouth
and breathing on the face of the victim, who was henceforth in the
creature's thrall.

Henna el-dabeah—its name embodying our fears and desires
as one. For henna, crushed into a paste from the dried leaves of

the *lawsonia alba*, is a symbol of sweetness and allure in the Arab world and is applied to the hands and feet of the bride-to-be as part of the wedding ceremony. Bending over the plant, Fathi had said, "The colors of the flower change in order to confuse insects." Then he added: "Darb el-henna w-darb el-shok," the sweet way and the bitter.

So how Greek was Meleager? Or to put it differently: being Syrian-born, would the poet have been the beneficiary of the cultural mix—"the hermaphroditic world where even the language spoken is an alloy," to quote Seferis on Cavafy[13]—of his surroundings? Gadara became a Greek polis in 218 BC under Antiochus the Great, but the origin of its name is probably Semitic, meaning in both Arabic (*jadar*) and Hebrew (*gader*) a fence bordering a road, its name and dramatic setting suggesting that the site was an ancient outpost. Antiochus decided to give the city the new name Antiochia Semiramis, but this didn't stick beyond his reign. It may be equally possible that mercenaries, sent to man a garrison in the Syrian highlands in the very early days of Seleucid domination of Asia, had named the stronghold to memorialize the Macedonian village of Gadeira. If so Meleager, son of Eukrates, could have descended from a soldier of fortune who had been awarded citizenship and property for services rendered to the royal house.

Then again Meleager might have come from a family of professionals who drifted from one Greek colony to another in pursuit of royal patronage. There were itinerant doctors and engineers, scholars and teachers, philosophers and architects, musicians and actors, as well as consuls and judges, arbitrators, and envoys to the court, commonly known as the sovereign's helpers, or "friends." One thing is certain, at least from the evidence of the extant poems: Meleager, as a Cynic and a Panhellene, would blithely turn his back on the political intrigues of the Seleucids, their civil wars, their disputes over territory with the Ptolemaic kingdoms in Egypt, and their efforts to fend off the Romans as well as the Hasmoneans of Judea.

No, Meleager's allegiances were of a different order altogether: he was, as he says of himself, a poet "who mixed sweet-speaking Graces with Eros and the Muses";[14] and the only strife to speak of in his verse was that of the soul—the fluttering psyche—smitten by the beauty of the likes of Heliodora, Kleoboulos and Mysikos, Theron, Alexis and Zenophila, stealing from his bed at dawn. Meleager's pledge to Eros encapsulated the Greek ideal of the good and the beautiful, *agathos kai kalos*, even as civil strife and the machinations of war shook the foundations of Hellenism in the East. Tucked away in the *Greek Anthology* is even a quatrain where Meleager laments the fact that his lover has spent the night with a Jew:

> Pale-cheeked Demo, someone's pinned you under
> in delight while my own heart groans within me.
> If he's bridled his longing for Sabbath, no great wonder;
> Love burns hot even on chilly Sabbaths.[15]

Perhaps it is in using the epithet "holy earth" for Gadara that Meleager betrays the Syriac in himself. He may simply be speaking of the aura of childhood haunts, but *xiera chthon* would also imply specific sites—groves and caves and springs—believed to be endowed with divine powers, such as the nymphaeum or sacred pool I had visited in the ruins of Gadara. Some sites were dedicated to the Greek gods, while others were consecrated to non-Greek Phoenician and Syrian deities such as Astarte, Atargatis, and Hadad, the first honored with considerable pomp at Heliopolis (Baalbek) in northern Syria.

Is this what Meleager meant when he wrote that the island of Cos "looked after [cherished] the old man in his age"? By then he had traveled a bit—from the Syrian highlands to the shores of Asia

Minor—and spoke of himself as a disciple of his fellow Gadarene Menippus, and as a cosmopolitan: "If [I am] a Syrian, what is the wonder? My friend, we inhabit a single homeland, the Cosmos; one Chaos gave birth to all mortals."[16] It is in Cos, dwelling on the skirts—so I imagine—of its famed sanctuary to Asclepios, the god of healing, that Meleager would have labored over the *Garland*, his anthology of epigrammatic poetry that served as the seedbed for what eventually evolved into the vast repository of Greek epigrams known as the *Palatine* or *Greek Anthology*. His preface, written in elegiacs, names forty-seven poets as contributors and brilliantly tags to each a choice flower. The result is a veritable botanical guide to the Mediterranean basin and as such illustrates how Meleager combined an intensely localized weave of flora with an altogether broader worldview, both cosmos and *koinos*—a "common tongue" to the initiated, the hellenismos:

> He put marjoram, the flower of Polystratos' songs, with them, and fresh Phoenician henna from Antipater; he added Syrian spikenard, the poet we sing of as "the gift of Hermes"; and the wild flowers of the corn-field, Poseidippos and Hedylos, and the anemones of Sikelidas. Yes, and the golden branch of the ever-divine Plato, everywhere bright with his skill; together with Aratos who knew the stars, cutting the first-grown branches from his heaven-high palm-tree.[17]

Callimachus, a favorite of Meleager's, whose flower was "sweet myrtle, always full of astringent honey,"[18] insisted that a poet keep to the back roads. According to Fathi the Arabic equivalent for this sort of wandering in the mind is *sarah*, "to pasture." So too in Hebrew the word for "idea" or "thought," *ra'ayon*, stems from the verb *ra'ah*, "to graze one's flock." This makes perfect sense, since both the ancient Hebrews and the Arabs sprang from the desert in search of pasture. They must have had their best thoughts while herding their livestock. The Peripatetics knew this to be true, as did Thoreau: "You must walk like a camel," he insists, "which is said to be the only beast which ruminates when walking."[19]

But I am about to enter the Hall of Inscriptions, which is why I brought Fathi and Mu'awiya to el-Hammeh in the first place. When Fathi had suggested a car trip to a place of my choosing, he instantly revived an old longing: Empress Eudocia, visiting the thermal springs in the fifth century, had left a dedicatory poem inscribed in Greek on a marble slab embedded in the floor of the Baths; and my secret design, in suggesting Hamat-Gader, had been to locate the poem of the Byzantine empress in situ.

My own introduction to Eudocia dates to the winter of 2000, when a friend and I were driving back to Jerusalem from Nablus in the West Bank, where we regularly met with a group of Palestinians. Judith, an archeologist and Hellenist, had published a study of Eudocia's poem, which included an English translation and line-by-line commentary. I'd taken Judith's paper with me to Gadara that same year in the hope of finding the inscription, but soon realized that the imperial paean to the mineral springs was located on the Israeli side of the Yarmuk stream. Eudocia would have to wait.

Six years later, almost to the day, I find myself stepping over rubble into Area D (according to the archeologists' floor plan of the thermae) a large, rectangular, unroofed hall built around a stepped pool with limestone niches and narrow extensions at both ends, and bordered by a row of squat marble fountains. This is the Hall of Fountains, also known as the Hall of Niches. Caper plants grow in profusion from cracks in the wall. A pair of scrub warblers hops about, their tails cocked high, in the far corner. I circle the pool, retracing my steps to the smaller Hall of Inscription, all the while scanning the high limestone walls, the recesses and pavement, and the ravaged, animal-faced fountains where water once spouted into the pool—and belatedly realize that such an inscription, running up to sixteen lines, would have been removed from the premises for safekeeping.

But Judith's paper was still with me, tucked into my copy of Whigham and Jay's *The Poems of Meleager* in my satchel. If Meleager had ever hiked to the hot springs, it would have been long before the construction of the hall I—a touch disappointed—was standing in. It was more likely that he'd have made his way down to the natural spring in Area G, behind the Oval Hall. I follow a footpath to the hottest of the sulfurous wellsprings—*ein makla*, "the frying pan"—half hidden in reeds and tamarisk bushes before retracing my steps to the thermae, past the small lepers' bath wedged between the Hall of Pillars and the Oval Hall, and, finding myself a seat on the edge of the pool in the Hall of Fountains, legs dangling over its weedy floor, I read the empress's encomium:

OF THE EMPRESS EUDOCIA

In my life many and infinite wonders have I seen.
But who, however many his mouths, could proclaim, O noble
    Clibanus,
Your strength, having been born a worthless mortal? But rather
It is fitting that you be called a new fiery ocean,
Paean and life source, provider of sweet streams.
From you is born the infinite swell, here one, there another,
On this side boiling, but there in turn cold and tepid.
You pour forth your beauty into four tetrads of springs.

Indian and Matrona, Repentinus, Elijah the Holy,
Antoninus the Good, dewy Galatia and
Hygieia herself, the large warm (baths) and the small warm
    (baths),
The Pearl, the old Clibanus, Indian, and also another
Matrona, Briara and the Nun, and the (spring) of the Patriarch.

For those in pain your mighty strength (is ever constant.)
But (I will sing) of god, famous for wisdom . . .
For the benefit of men . . .[20]

The proper nouns, pagan and Christian, that had confused
me in the confines of my study when I first read the poem now
make perfect sense: Eudocia is leading us by the hand, as it were,
through the complex of baths that must have functioned as a
therapeutic-cult center for the mixed population of non-Christians
as well as the recently converted. The exotic-sounding names in
the second stanza would have belonged to the individual baths, or
to the statues decorating the niches, or even to the row of fountains, which one archeologist suggests might have been installed
by the empress as a new addition to the baths.

Eudocia, née Athenais, was the daughter of the itinerant soph-
ist Leontius, and became a devout Christian only after moving to
Constantinople and marrying Theodosius II in 421. As the poem
demonstrates, she moved between the pagan and Christian worlds
with consummate ease. The Homeric echoes are there right from
the start: "But the multitude I could not tell nor name, / No, not
though ten tongues were mine and ten mouths" (*Iliad*, book 2,
lines 488–89), and lines 6–8 recall Calypso's magic cave: "And
fountains four in a row were flowing with bright water / Hard by
one another, turned one this way, one that." In the encomium's
very first line Eudocia might have had in mind another cave scene,
that of the nymphs in book 13 of the *Odyssey*, where *thauma ides-
thai*, "a wonder to see," chimes with *thaumt' opopa*, "wonders I
have seen," especially as Homer's following line reads, "the water
flows unceasingly" (lines 108–9), which is picked up by Eudocia:
"from you is born the infinite swell." Given her solid grounding
in classical literature, there is a good chance Eudocia would have
been familiar with Porphyry of Tyre's Neoplatonic essay on the
Cave of the Nymphs. He too had studied in Athens before moving

to Rome during the first half of the third century, and his reading of Homer was keenly allegorical, a position Eudocia would adapt in her own theistic treatment of pagan themes. Here is Porphyry on line 108, "weave sea-purple cloth, a wonder to see":

> The sea-purple cloth would clearly be the flesh, woven of blood: the sea-purple wool, the fiber itself, is ultimately the product of blood and the wool is even dyed with a product derived from living creatures. Likewise, the production of flesh is accomplished both by blood and out of blood. Moreover, the body surely is a cloak for the soul around which it is wrapped, "a wonder to see" whether you consider it from the point of view of the composition of the composite entity or from that of the soul's bondage to the body. Thus, according to Orpheus, Kore, the overseer of all things sown in the earth, is depicted as a weaver, and the ancients called heaven a "robe," as if it were a garment cast around the heavenly gods.[21]

For Porphyry, the disciple and biographer of Plotinus, the *Odyssey* was to be read as a journey of the soul toward moral excellence, purity, and wisdom. This, I believe, is precisely how Eudocia read her Homer. For she lived in the wake of an era in which the early church fathers, such as Origen of Alexandria and the Cappadocians Basil of Caesarea and Gregory Nazianzus, were intent on showing how the teachings of Christ were in essence an extension of Hellenism. Homer would be read in the light of the new *paideia*, the divine logos of which he was, along with Plato, the great precursor. "But (I will sing) of god, famous for wisdom," ends Empress Eudocia's encomium, where the Greek *klutometis*, "famous in skill," was a common epithet for Hephaestus as well as for Asklepios.

We find ourselves once again in that "hermaphroditic" world of late antiquity—that twilight zone where Hellenism, pagan

Mystery cults, and the aftershocks of a new dispensation all converge. And sitting in the Hall of Inscriptions as the sun beats down on the nape of my neck, trying to make sense of the different plans of the baths—Roman and Byzantine, and Umayyad-Abbasid—each with its own renovations, its own extensions and embellishments and commemorating inscriptions, it no longer seems surprising that a Byzantine empress should have written a poem in hexameters in praise of "noble Clibanus," the furnace that regulated the temperature of the hot springs of el-Hammeh, which is likened to Paean, the physician of the gods. After all, Eudocia had also written, while living in Jerusalem, a verse paraphrase of the Bible entirely composed stitched—of lines from Homer. Of Eve's disobedience, Eudocia writes via Homer:

> She unwittingly did a monstrous deed, (*Odyssey* 11.272)
> And, destructive, she wrought many evils for men;
>   *Odyssey* 17.287)
> She cast many strong souls to Hades' abode, (*Iliad* 1.3)
> Wrought hardship for all, caused trouble for many.[22]
>   (*Iliad* 21.524)

The popularity of Eudocia's *Homeric Centos* was short-lived. It was vilified by St. Jerome, who called it *puerilia* and "like the games of itinerant tricksters,"[23] and, closer to our own times, ridiculed, as in Elizabeth Barrett Browning's delightfully exasperated vignette: "There she sat among the ruins of the holy city, addressing herself most unholily, with whatever good intentions and delicate fingers, to pulling Homer's gold to pieces bit by bit. . . . The reader, who has heard enough of centos, will not care to hear how she did it. That she did it was too much; and the deed recoiled."[24] Yet sitting among the ruins of the Roman Baths I can't help feeling gratitude toward Eudocia and her art, her patchwork stitchings (centos) of double-entendres, which translate back into Greek as "rhapsody" and forward into the language of our own times as high modernism—intertextual, syncretic, transgressive—*avant la lettre*.

* * *

Over the centuries pilgrims, mystics, and sages as well as the crippled, healers, and theurgists and plain curiosity seekers and picnickers would visit the mineral springs. By far, however, the most remarkable report comes from the pen of Eunapius, a disciple of the third- to fourth-century Syrian neo-Pythagorean Iamblichus, who had been a pupil of Porphyry. Eunapius recounts how one day Theois Iamblichos, "the Divine Iamblichus," urged by his pupils to show them his theurgical powers, set out together with his followers for Gadara, "a place which has warm baths in the area"; while bathing, his followers again insisted he give them a sign, a *synthemata* of the divine nature of the soul, at which point he conceded and asked them to verify the name of the two hot springs. They said:

> "There is no pretense about it, this spring is called Eros, and the name of the one next to it is Anteros." He at once touched the water with his hand—he happened to be sitting on the ledge of the spring where the overflow runs off—and uttering a brief summons he called forth a boy from the depth of the spring. He was white skinned and of medium height, his locks were golden and his back and breast shone; and he exactly resembled one who was bathing or had just bathed. His disciples were overwhelmed with amazement, but Iamblichus said, "let us go to the next spring," and he rose and led the way, with a thoughtful air. Then he went through the same performance there also, and summoned another Eros like the first in all respects, except that his hair was darker and fell loose in the sun. Both the boys embraced Iamblichus and clung

closely to him as though he were a real father. He restored them to their proper places and went away after his bath, reverenced by his pupils.[25]

It is time, to be sure, to get back to Fathi and Mu'awiya, who must be getting tired of the mineral pools. I'd forgotten, however, that Judith's paper dealt with two additional inscriptions, which I can't help reading before I take leave of the ruins. The first dates from the late fifth to early sixth century and concerns a donation for the construction of a vaulted bath or *tholos* by one Alexander of Caesarea; but it is the second inscription that now has me smiling and quickens my pace back to the spa. Fathi is sunk, rotund and content as a walrus, in his deck chair. Mu'awiya, he tells me, has gone off to the "splash coldwater pool" to check out the giant water slide. I have something to show them, I announce, and go off to fetch his son.

Mu'awiya waves from the top of the slide, then disappears into its spiraling tunnel. For a split second his silhouette, perched to shoot out of the tube with a splash, is projected against the fiberglass of the slide's lip. Two more torpedo runs and Mu'awiya and I follow the path back to the thermal pools.

The Greek inscription, I explain to father and son, was found in the old Roman baths I'd been exploring for the last hour. I translate the English version into a mixture of Hebrew and Arabic:

In the days of Abd Allah Mu'awiya, the commander of the faithful, the hot baths of the people there were saved and rebuilt by Abd Allah son of Abuasemos (Abu Hasim) the Counsellor, on the fifth of the month of December, on the second day, in the sixth year of the indiction, in the year 726 of the colony, according to the Arabs the forty-second year, for the healing of the sick, under the care of Ioannes, the official of Gadara.[26]

Fathi gives off one of his gleeful snorts. Mu'awiya ibn Abi Sufyan, he reminds me, was the first caliph of the Umayyad dynasty, which ruled from Damascus. The forty-second year, Fathi makes a quick calculation, would have been 662, one year after the caliph came to power. He was, Fathi adds, the Herod of the Arab world, as regards major building projects—palaces, mosques, monuments—so why not restore el-Hammeh as well. Besides, his son Yazid suffered from swollen feet and would definitely have benefited from the baths. I'm not sure whether Fathi is pulling my leg, for even as he speaks an enormous dropsical bather in blue goggles and a faded pink bathrobe waddles by.

I'm reminded of yet another story Fathi told me the other day about the caliph. We had retired after supper to the wood-burner he'd built against the side of his home, and where he would remove himself regularly at dusk to prepare, Arab-style, in three separate long-beaked pots, his roasted, home-brewed *qahwe*. This little corner of his, giving onto the neighbor's lemon trees and a step away from his son's goat pen, was, I came to realize, his own *arrière-boutique*, or back shop, where he could go out to pasture, in a manner of speaking—*sarah*—in his mind. "Mu'awiya," he told me, as he poked at the dying embers under the burnished coffee pots, "was a wise man who ruled his people by the thread of a hair. 'When they pull,' he would say, 'I loosen, and when they loosen, I pull.'"

His son wants to know why the inscription isn't written in Arabic. Fathi too is surprised, but explains that Palestine was Byzantine at the time, and Greek was probably what people used in the *sūq* (market). "Maybe this guy Abd wanted to impress the locals." Mu'awiya isn't unduly impressed by his namesake's inscription and slips away while I translate for his father the opening lines of Eudocia's poem.

"So who was this lady-poet?" he asks, leaning out of his lounge chair.

"Well, for one she was the wife of an emperor."

"How did she get here? Maybe she also had swollen feet."

"Actually, as the story goes it had more to do with an apple."

"An apple?"

"Of unusual size given to her by her husband, Theodosius II. For some reason she offers the apple to a court official named Paulinus, who unwittingly presents it as a gift to the emperor. Theodosius II immediately suspects foul play and summons his wife to account for her actions."

"What does she say?"

"She insists she ate the apple. Not a very good move, as the emperor is now convinced the apple was given to Paulinus as a token of love. And to add spice to the story, tradition has it that Theodosius and Paulinus were childhood friends. The distraught emperor has Paulinus summarily executed, and the humiliated empress, deemed guilty by the public, sets out on a pilgrimage to the Holy Land."

"So that's how she gets to Hamat Gader?"

"Well, yes and no."

Fathi suggests we take one last dip, and I continue my tale as we wade into the steaming pool.

"She did come to Palestine," I told him. "In 438 and again in 442, when permanently estranged from the emperor. She remained in Jerusalem until her death in 460. But her motives for leaving Constantinople may have had less to do with an apple than with her sister-in-law Pulcheria. Theodosius II's sister wielded considerable power in the imperial court—in fact she too was an empress, and behind the simple narrative there lies a tale of Byzantine intrigue."

We're up to our necks in the deep end, lightly treading water and occasionally bouncing against the bottom of the pool. Fathi wants to know more. I suggest we return to the shallow end of the pool.

"It boils down to a pair of strong-headed women vying for power and for the attention of the emperor. The sister Pulcheria, older, more experienced than her brother, and extremely, even fanatically pious, had chosen Eudocia as the perfect consort for Theodosius II. Eudocia was both beautiful and learned, and the latter trait, her learning, was a quality she would share with her future husband, who had a scholarly bent, while it also, in the end, deepened the rift between the two empresses.

"Eudocia was the daughter of a philosopher. As such she knew her astronomy and geometry, grammar, literature, and philosophy. In short she was a Hellene who brought to her conversion the full weight of her classical education. Her sister-in-law, on the other hand, belonged to the new orthodoxy. She'd made a vow of chastity, founded new churches, campaigned for the translation of holy relics to Constantinople, and in the disputes raging at the time between those bishops who believed Mary was the Mother of God and those who insisted she was the Mother of Christ, Pulcheria firmly belonged to the former, more fanatical camp."

Fathi is looking at me in disbelief. He himself has confessed earlier that he isn't exactly a practicing Muslim, even though the muezzin across the street wakes him up at dawn every day to remind him of his obligations to Allah.

"But the story isn't quite done, Fathi."

"Let's at least get our backs tickled."

We wade back to the far side of the pool. Each chooses his own private jet of water, and I go on:

"I don't think Eudocia took to Pulcheria's brand of religion, and vice versa. But in the early years Eudocia's pagan background didn't matter much, as her sister-in-law was pulling the strings in the imperial palace. All comes to a head when Eudocia sets out for Palestine in 438, visits the holy shrines, kneels at Christ's tomb, and returns to Constantinople as the new Helena."

"Constantine's mother."

"A model of Christian piety. So Eudocia's popularity soars, and soon enough she's appointing her own favorites to key positions in court. Pulcheria becomes increasingly distraught and jealous. Not only was she losing her power base and her hold on her weak-willed brother, but the church was being led astray by a false piety, perhaps even by crypto-pagans who did not believe in Christ's absolute divinity."

"In the Koran Allah snatches Christ from the cross because he wants to safeguard his body and soul intact. The body bleeding on the cross is only a likeness, a semblance of Jesus," Fathi chimes in.

"The bishops of Byzantium would get into fistfights over how exactly God had joined man to or *in* Christ."

"But did she or didn't she?"

"Did who? What?"

"Eudocia. Did she sleep with Paulinus?"

"Rumors were spread by a eunuch named Chrysaphius, who figured the best way to become the emperor's right hand was to rid himself of the empresses. First he managed to get Pulcheria to retreat to a convent outside the city, and then he charged Eudocia with adultery. The emperor swallowed the bait, and the damage was done. Exile in Jerusalem—which apparently had made a deep impression during her first visit—was her only way out."

"Neveradullmoment!" Fathi exclaims in English in one breath as we make for our chairs by the poolside. It was a phrase he'd jotted down one morning at breakfast in the pocket-size notebook I'd bought him in Jerusalem after he'd commented on my zealous note taking. From then on I was no longer the sole recipient of words and popular sayings and fragments of song, as Fathi filled the pages of his new notebook with the old English saws I managed to dredge up from memory. Never a dull . . . A penny saved . . . seemed embarrassingly dull in comparison to Fathi's endless supply of folk wisdom. I couldn't understand why he would want to write down lines I half-remembered from my scouting days, "Pack up your troubles in your old kit bag and smile, smile, smile," after he'd sung to me a lovely couplet from a Lebanese popular song:

mala sanabil tanhani bitawdu
wal farerat rusu hona shawamhu

(the full ear of wheat bows in modesty
while the empty stands high and lofty)

"There's just one more little detail about Eudocia that I forgot to mention," I tell Fathi after skimming through my notebook to where I'd copied down excerpts from a chronicle of the empress's visit to Jerusalem, as well as an anonymous poem appearing in the *Greek Anthology* about her first visit to the city:

The wise mistress of the world,
enflamed by pious love, comes as a servant,
and she who is worshipped by all worships the tomb of One.
For He who gave her a husband and a throne,
died as a man but lives a God;
below he played the man, but above He was as He was.[27]

"You won't believe this, but in the spring of 438 Eudocia actually sprained her ankle while visiting a shrine on the Mount of Olives. The chronicler Gerontius claims it was 'by the devil's malignity.' So maybe you're right, and she did travel to the springs because of a swollen ankle."

Fathi is delighted at the thought of the empress hobbling all the way to el-Hammeh to soak her ankle in the mineral springs. He asks to look at my notebook, flips through its pages, and notices a pencil drawing on the inside cover, with the date scribbled on the upper left-hand corner.

The little notebook with its brown mottled cover and green spine, I explain, had belonged to a friend of mine who died in 1998. I'd found it among his belongings, its pages blank except for the squiggles on the inside of the cardboard cover. I'd decided before leaving for the Galilee that after all these years, it was time fill its pages. Dennis Silk was no relation of James Silk Buckingham, who had visited Hamat Gader in 1816, though he had apparently wished to be so; and in "Tryphon," a fabulist account of the latter's travels to Palestine published in *Encounter* in the late sixties, he had "revived the embers of James Buckingham Silk." Curiously enough, Tryphon the giant Chimera is described as a funambulist who "circumscribed Jerusalem on a skipping-rope suspended in mid-air."[28] So it may well be that in "skipping-rope blues," with *hesed* and *din*, the Hebrew words for "mercy" and "judgment" or "justice" at either end of the rope, Dennis was toying with a notion of his that originated in the image of Tryphon. As a practitioner of Thing Theater, he had tenaciously held on to a handful of such simple pictorial notions for a lifetime—like the spiral he'd doodle under his name ever since the time he'd spent in Malta as a young man and had traced with his fingers the spirals covering the walls of the Stone Age megaliths on the island. Somewhere Camus speaks of a man's long journey to retrieve two or three images whose presence first opens the heart. Much later, when Dennis knew he was dying of a blood cancer, he would write in "Spiral Kasida," a long prose poem: "a bad spiral takes him down with the last whirl-ward of it."

"Skipping-rope blues," Fathi pronounces, before copying the phrase into his own notebook. I'm not sure how to translate *blues* into Arabic, or for that matter into Hebrew. What were the words Fathi used when speaking of Fairuz's Andalusian songs? Her

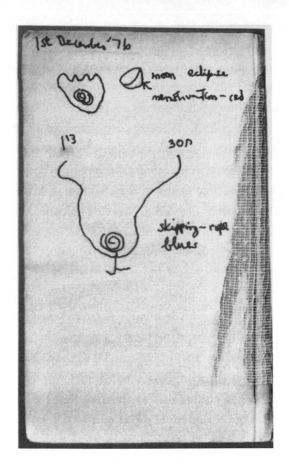

songs were blended (*mahool*) in his heart, like wine mixed with water with a pinch of *huzn*, sadness. Had there been an eclipse on December 1, 1976, and might the words *menstruation—red* refer to the atmospheric effect of the full moon's passage through the earth's shadow? Its coppery-red hue? Menstruation—from the Greek *mene* (moon)—its cycles coinciding with the rhythm of the lunar phases. Was this what Dennis was working out in his squiggles? Had he fallen under the spell of some ancient, Near Eastern symbolism, where a spiral-faced stick figure balanced Justice and Mercy under an umbral eclipse?

"*Yalla*, it's time to go." Fathi's good humor snaps me out of the windings of my own thoughts. Before it gets dark he wants to retrieve the two burlap sacks of wheat we'd dropped off in the morning at the single-pump station. We pick up Mu'awiya at the coldwater pool and follow the arrows to the park entrance. Not far from the remains of the Roman amphitheater stands a booth where you can have your photo taken while holding a live iguana. Mu'awiya cradles the pet and smiles into the camera, radiant. We then make a quick tour of the animal farm, including the crocodile ponds, where we meet up with the husband and wife from Baqa el-Gharbiyyeh. They're lagging behind a large, ragtag group led by a voluble tour guide. Fathi whispers to me, as we're staring at a crocodile's open jaws jutting out of the water, that it's one of the excursions organized by the Ministry of Defense for parents who've lost a son or daughter during military service or in acts of terror. Probably the latter, Fathi suggests, given the presence of the couple from Baqa el-Gharbiyyeh, unless they are Druze or Bedouin, in which case their child might have served in the IDF. It's the skipping-rope blues, Fathi adds, as the crocodile snaps its jaws shut.

On the way out I suggest we take a quick look at the mosaic floor of the ancient synagogue I'd read about in Sukenik's paper. Mu'awiya and his father opt for the parrot show that's about to start while I set out to find the synagogue. Oddly enough nobody seems to know of the site's existence. Several years ago I'd visited Beth Alpha in the Jordan Valley, a synagogue from late antiquity that Sukenik had uncovered in 1929, with a mosaic floor executed in what had seemed at first glance to be a childlike, primitive style. Subsequently I learned that the remains of such floor mosaics—more often than not badly defaced by iconoclasts—were scattered throughout the Levant. Apparently these rustic mosaics had been laid by provincial, itinerant artists, not unlike the painter from Gaza who had showed up one day at Fathi's home and had turned his living room wall into a Swiss meadow, with snow-capped mountains in the background and an Arab *fallah* in the foreground, leaning on a grub hoe by a brook.

The painter from Gaza, who according to Fathi had proceeded to brush onto the walls of some two dozen more homes in Sakhnin his particular vision of the meeting of the East and the West, had a glancing knowledge of perspective and color values. In the same way, the artists of Beth Alpha—Marianos and his son Hanina, as they are identified in Greek—must have been familiar with the mosaics of the larger cities in the region, such as Gadara and Madaba in Transjordan; Scythopolis, Sepphoris, and Caesarea in Palestine; and, further north, Antioch and Dura-Europa. However stiffly the figures may have been rendered, father and son had evidently relished the opportunity to draw upon both Jewish and pagan iconography: the Ark of the Covenant, the Greek Zodiac (with a central disc depicting Helios in his chariot led by four horses), and the story of the Sacrifice of Isaac. Hellenism, or at least its mythography, had continued to fascinate the varied population of Byzantine and Umayyad Palestine.

Beth Alpha had proved to be another example of the exceptional amalgamation of traditions in the Levant, and in seeking out the Byzantine synagogue of Hamat Gader I was firmly back on my old hobbyhorse. "In the centre of the southern panel, in front of the apse," writes Sukenik,

There is an inscription [in Aramaic] of ten lines enclosed in a wreath. The wreath is tied at the bottom with a red cord in a neat bow having two loops. The ends of the cord fall gracefully below and to the sides, and terminate in ivy leaves. The upper left side of the inscription, as well as the adjacent portion of the mosaic, has suffered considerably from the fire which once burnt the synagogue and blackened the tesserae. The inscription is flanked by lions with heavy manes, tails gracefully held above their backs with the tips bent backward, and red tongues protruding. The animals are represented in motion, having just taken a step forward with the leg that is farther from the observer, against which the genitals are exposed.[29]

These were not your run-of-the-mill Lions of Judah. According to Sukenik, the synagogue was erected no later than the first half of the fifth century, and I fancy Empress Eudocia had a nodding acquaintance with the priapic pair, which I am now at pains to locate. After all, she was reported to have staunchly supported the Jews of Byzantine Palestine, in contrast to her rival Pulcheria and her erstwhile husband Theodosius II, who issued (in her absence) one edict after another aimed at embittering—and endangering— the lives of pagans, Samaritans, and Jews alike.

According to Sukenik's map of the plain of el-Hammeh, the basilica-shaped synagogue stood on a mound called Tell Bani. Apart from the amphitheater, the only mound in sight rises behind the Spa Village Hotel and is topped by a rusty military watchtower. I cut through the sloping grove of old ficus trees where we'd picnicked earlier and follow a goat path to the crest of the flat-topped mound that is covered in brambles and the salty-leaved orache bush, familiar to me from the path that once led to Silk's shack overlooking the walls of Jerusalem's Old City. Traces of a basalt wall and broken pieces of an antique column protrude from the underbrush, but before I have a chance to poke around any further a female voice assuming a gruff tone calls out from the camouflaged tower: "Hey! What are you doing here?" "I'm looking for an old synagogue," I call back to the voice, instantly realizing how ridiculous I must sound.

"Wait a minute." A slip of a girl in an oversize uniform clambers down the watchtower ladder. "This is a military zone," she explains, pointing at the barbed-wire fence that separates us from the Hashemite Kingdom, a mere ten paces away. I take out Sukenik's survey and tell her about my efforts to locate the ancient synagogue of el-Hammeh. "I think we're standing on its ruins," I say.

"You're kidding."

"No, look, this must be Tell Bani." We bend over Sukenik's map. Plain, mound, and river at the bottom of the narrowing gorge correspond perfectly with the archeologist's drawing. I then show her an illustration of the mosaic floor. Her eyes widen at the sight of the lions, who look more dazed than menacing. "That's something," she says, smiling. Her name is Shiran, and she's bored out of her mind from sitting in the watchtower all day. I ask her if she minds my poking around the ruins. "No, if you're already here." Shiran climbs back up into her perch, and I cautiously negotiate through the brake. It's been close to eighty years since Sukenik excavated Tell Bani, and time has long reburied the ancient synagogue in fresh layers of dirt and prickly scrub and underbrush.

Finally I circle back and wave to the young recruit—or at least to her shadow moving about behind camouflage, as the air fills with crackles and squelches coming from the shortwave in the tower. Fathi and Mu'awiya are waiting for me by the entrance to Hamat Gader. They describe the parrot show, which included macaws and cockatoos push-pedaling across a tightrope on toy unicycles. Fathi has our next trip all lined up for us. As he backs out of the parking lot he proposes that we hire a pair of donkeys from a friend of his and explore the Golan Heights at the easy pace of the long-eared beasts of burden. And what about the mosaics you were looking for? he asks. I tell him they're buried under a watchtower manned by a dark-eyed houri named Shiran. Meleager might have called her Heliodora, Gift of the Sun.

NOTES

PREFACE

1 For the history of Ein Hawd/Ein Hod and the continued plight of its original inhabitants, or internal refugees, see Meron Benvenisti, *Sacred Landscape: The Buried History of the Holy Land since 1948* (Berkeley: University of California Press, 2000), pp. 193–200.

2 See Adina Hoffman, *My Happiness Bears No Relation to Happiness: A Poet's Life in the Palestinian Century* (New Haven, Ct: Yale University Press, 2009), pp. 265–79 for a moving account of Hussein's participation in the tumultuous first meeting between Arab and Jewish writers in 1958 and his tragic death in New York City.

3 My adaptation of *kinnus* (ingathering), the term used by H. N. Bialik for the retrievement of Jewish literary culture, notably in his coediting, with J. H. Ravnitsky, of *Sefer Ha-Aggadah* [The Book of Legends] and of the Medieval Hebrew poets Shlomo Ibn Gabirol and Moshe Ibn Ezra.

4 From "Davar" [Word], in C. N. Bialik, *Kol Shirei Bialik* [The Complete Poems] (Tel Aviv: Dvir, 1972), p. 172.

5 Aminadav A. Dykman's explication of "To the Sun," in *Reading Hebrew Literature: Critical Discussions of Six Modern Texts*, ed. Alan Mintz (Hanover, NH: University Press of New England / Brandeis University Press, 2003) pp. 73–80.

6 See Yaacov Shavit, *The Hebrew Nation: A Study in Israeli Heresy and Fantasy* (London: Frank Cass, 1987).

7 Danziger sojourned in Paris in the early fifties, at which time he met my grandfather, Marek Szwarc, a Polish Jew, sculptor, and painter, who had converted to Roman Catholicism in 1919. The two would frequent the Near Eastern galleries of the Louvre together and, as the story goes, were once scolded by a guard for "fondling the statues." Danziger, who was to become a forerunner of environmental and site-specific art in Israel, was killed in a car accident in 1977, the same year that Rashid Hussein, another outlander, died of smoke inhalation when his New York City apartment went up in flames.

8 See Deborah A. Starr and Sasson Somekh, eds., *Mongrels or Marvels: The Levantine Writings of Jacqueline Shohet Kahanoff* (Stanford, CA: Stanford University Press, 2011).

9 Paul Celan, "The Meridian," in *Collected Prose*, trans. Rosmarie Waldrop (New York: Sheep Meadow Press, 1986), pp. 44, 46.

10 Victor Segalen, trans. and ed. by Yael Rachel Schlick, *Essay on Exoticism: An Aesthetics of Diversity* (Durham, NC: Duke University Press, 2002), p. 61.

11 Ibid., p. 16.

12 Full translation in Gabriel Levin, *The Maltese Dreambook* (London: Anvil, 2008), pp. 53–58.

CHAPTER ONE

1 *The Selected Poems of Frank O'Hara*, ed. Donald Allen (New York: Vintage Books, 1994), p. xiii.

2 D. H. Lawrence, *Studies in Classic American Literature* (Middlesex: Penguin Books, 1971), p. 181.

3 Genesis 12:1.

4 "The Descent of Inanna," in *Inanna, Queen of Heaven and Earth: Her Stories and Hymns from Sumer*, trans. Diane Wolkstein and Samuel Kramer (New York: Harper and Row, 1983), p. 52.

5 Ibid., p. 60.

6 Ibid., pp. 88–89.

7 *The Epic of Gilgamesh*, trans. and ed. Benjamin R. Foster, Norton Critical Edition (New York: W. W. Norton, 2001), p. 135.

8 George Seferis, *Collected Poems 1924–1955*, trans., ed., and introduced by Edmund Keeley and Philip Sherrard (London: Jonathan Cape, 1973), p. 7.

9 Robert Duncan, "A Poem Beginning with a Line by Pindar," in *The Opening of the Field* (New York: New Directions, 1960), p. 65.

10 From *The Cantos of Ezra Pound* (New York: New Directions, 1986), pp. 795–96.

11 Hawthorne's complete account of Melville's visit is cited in Herman Melville, *Journals* (Evanston, IL: Northwestern University Press; Chicago: Newberry Library, 1993), 14:628.

12 Ibid., 15:80.

13 Ibid., 15:89.

14 Ibid., 15:83.

15 Herman Melville, *Correspondence* (Evanston, IL: Northwestern University Press; Chicago: Newberry Library, 1993), 14:212.

16 Melville, *Journals*, 15:84.

17 Ibid., p. 86.

18 Ibid., p. 83.

19 Melville, *Correspondence*, 14:483.

20 Dennis Silk, *The Punished Land* (New York: Penguin Books, 1980), p. 18.

21   Jay Leyda, ed., *The Melville Log: A Documentary Life of Herman Melville, 1819–1891* (New York: Gordian Press, 1969), 2:747.

22   Andrew Delbanco, *Melville: His World and Work* (New York: Vintage Books, 2006), p. 279.

23   Herman Melville, *Clarel* (Evanston, IL: Northwestern University Press; Chicago: Newberry Library, 1991), 12:489.

24   Ibid., 12:170.

25   Ezra Pound, *Selected Prose 1909–1965*, ed. with an introduction by William Cookson (London: Faber and Faber, 1973), p. 21.

26   Herman Melville, *Correspondence*, 14:121.

27   Paul Celan, "The Meridian," in *Collected Prose*, trans. Rosmarie Waldrop (New York: Sheep Meadow Press, 1986), p. 44.

28   Primo Levi, *Survival in Auschwitz* (New York: Touchstone Edition, 1996), p. 109.

29   Ibid., p. 112.

30   Ibid., p. 113.

31   Ibid., p. 114.

32   Ibid.

33   Ibid., p. 186.

34   T. S. Eliot, *Four Quartets* (London: Faber and Faber, 1955), p. 19.

35   See R. A. Nicholson, *A Literary History of the Arabs* (Cambridge: Cambridge University Press, 1976), p. 105.

36   Full translation in Gabriel Levin, *The Maltese Dreambook* (London: Anvil, 2008), pp. 53–58.

37   Ibid., pp. 53–54.

38   Zuhair, quoted in *The Works of Sir William Jones* (London: Printed for G. G. and J. Robonson, Pater-Noster-Row and R. H. Evans, 1799), 4:281.

39   Jorge Luis Borges, "Averroës' Search," in *Collected Fictions*, trans. Andrew Hurley (London: Penguin Books, 1998), p. 240.

40   Adonis, *An Introduction to Arab Poetics*, trans. Catherine Cobham (Austin: University of Texas Press, 1990), p. 34.

41   Levin, *The Maltese Dreambook*, pp. 57–58.

42   Stéphane Mallarmé, *Oeuvres Complètes* (Paris: Gallimard, 1998), 1:788.

43   Stéphane Mallarmé, *The Collected Poems*, trans. and with a commentary by Henry Weinfield (Berkeley: University of California Press, 1994), p. 126.

44   Tarafa, in *The Seven Odes*, trans. A. J. Arberry (London: Macmillan, 1957), p. 83.

45   Melville, *Clarel*, 12:169.

46   From Stéphane Mallarmé's letter to Villiers de l'Isle-Adam, September 24, 1866, in *Mallarmé: Selected Prose Poems, Essays, & Letters*, trans. Bradford Cook (Baltimore: John Hopkins University Press, 1957), p. 91.

47   Levin, *The Maltese Dreambook*, p. 55.

48   T. S. Eliot, *Collected Poems* (London: Faber and Faber, 1980), p. 78.

49   Jaroslav Stetkevych, *The Zephyrs of Najd: The Poetics of Nostalgia in the Classical Arabic Nasib* (Chicago: University of Chicago Press, 1993), pp. 16–26.

50   Harold Schimmel, *AR'A* (Tel Aviv: Siphrai Siman Kriyah, 1979), pp. 53–55.

51   Harold Schimmel, "Historical Grit & Epic Gestation," *Sagetrieb* 1, no. 2 (Fall 1982): 223.

52   Harold Schimmel, *Qasida*, trans. Peter Cole (Jerusalem: Ibis Editions, 1997), pp. 13, 14, 29, 33, 38, 43, 71–72.

53   Full English version appears in Harold Schimmel, *From Island to Island*, trans. Peter Cole (Jerusalem: Ibis Editions, 1997), pp. 42–43.

54   Antara, *The Seven Odes*, trans. A. J. Arberry (London: Macmillan, 1957), p. 179.

55   Schimmel, *From Island to Island*, pp. 45–46.

56   Ibid., p. 50.

57   Schimmel, *AR'A*, p. 6. My translation.

58   Harold Schimmel, "Zuk. Yehoash David Rex," in *Louis Zukofsky: Man and Poet*, ed. with an introduction by Carroll F. Terrell (Orono, ME: National Poetry Foundation, 1979), p. 238.

59   Schimmel, *From Island to Island*, pp. 56–57.

60   Al-Jahiz is reputed to have authored over two hundred highly eclectic titles (for the most part lost), ranging from the didactic-theological to the quasi-scientific (notably, *Kitab al-hayawan* [*The Book of Animals*]) and the literary—namely, moral instruction and etiquette; though how many of his tracts and epistles were of his own hand and how many should be read as apocryphal texts, forgeries, and misattributions has yet to be determined. For a taste of al-Jahiz's mocking, ribald tone, here is the preamble to the *Book of Misers*: "[In this book] I explain why misers describe avarice as 'thrift' and meanness as 'frugality'; why they enjoy saying 'no,' and make it out to be a sign of strength; why they are opposed to charity, which they equate with wastefulness; why they regard good works as extravagance and altruism as foolishness; why they have lost interest in praise, are little disturbed by criticism, despise those who enjoy being praised and like giving to others, and admire [eccentrics] who are concerned neither to win popularity nor to avoid blame. . . . You ask me to explain what it is that has clouded their minds, warped their understanding and made them blind and unbalanced. [You beg me to tell you] why they resist the truth and deny the obvious, [to analyze] this incongruity of temperament, this contradiction of character, in which crass foolishness rubs shoulders with surprising brilliance, [and to show you] why they grasp the details, which are obscure, while missing the whole, which is plain to see." From *The Life and Works of Jahiẓ*, ed. Charles Pellat, trans. from the French by D. M. Hawke (London: Routledge and Kegan Paul, 1969), pp. 236–37.

61   Stéphane Mallarmé, "Music and Letters" [La musique et les letters], trans. Rosemary Lloyd, in *Mallarmé in Prose*, ed. Mary Ann Caws (New York: New Directions, 2001), pp. 37–38.

62   "Jahan Serenades a Snake," in Eric Ormsby, *Araby*, Signal Editions (Montreal: Véhicule Press, 2001), p. 21.

63   Abdelfattah Kilito, *The Author & His Doubles: Essays on Classical Arabic*

Culture, trans. Michael Cooperson (Syracuse, NY: Syracuse University Press, 2001), pp.15–16.

64 My translation, adapted from *Early Arabic Poetry: Marathi and Su'luk Poems*, ed., trans., and commentary by Alan Jones, Oxford Oriental Monographs, no. 14 (Oxford: Oxford University Press, 1992), 1:153.

65 Jorge Luis Borges, "The Translators of The Thousand and One Nights," trans. Esther Allen, in *The Total Library: Nonfiction 1922–1986*, ed. Eliot Weinberger (New York, Penguin Books, 1999), p. 106.

66 John Ashbery, *Self-Portrait in a Convex Mirror* (New York: Viking Press, 1975), p. 9.

67 Ibid.

68 In Allen, *The Selected Poems of Frank O'Hara*, p. xiv.

69 Ibid., p. 105.

70 Ibid., p. 105.

71 Michael Sells, "The Mu'allaqa of Tarafa," *Journal of Arabic Literature* 17 (1986): 22.

72 Allen, *The Selected Poems of Frank O'Hara*, p. 107.

73 Ibid., p. 105.

74 George Oppen's *Primitive*, written late in life and subsequent to visiting the Qumran Caves at the Dead Sea on a trip to Israel in 1975, is another example of a collection in which topographies overlap in a final statement, part allegory, part narrative, of the poet's life journey. For an account of Mary and George Oppen's descent to the Dead Sea in 1975, see Shirley Kaufman, "The Obvious and the Hidden: Some Thoughts about 'Disasters,'" in *George Oppen: A Special Issue*, ed. Michael Cuddihy; *Ironwood* 26 (1985): 152–58.

75 Allen, *The Selected Poems of Frank O'Hara*, p. 106.

76 Schimmel, *Qasida*, p. 65.

77 Allen, *The Selected Poems of Frank O'Hara*, p. 106.

78 Ibid., p. 107.

79 Ibid., p. 108.

80 Ibid., p. 109.

81 Ibid.

82 Ibid., p. 110.

CHAPTER TWO

1 See Yehoshua Ben-Arieh, *Jerusalem in the 19th Century* (Jerusalem: Yad Izhak Ben-Zvi; New York: St. Martin's Press, 1986), p. 78.

2 Isaiah 17:5.

3 Job 26:5.

4 Joshua 5:9.

5 Noah Stern, *Ben Arphelim* [Amid Fogs]: *Poems, Translations, Prose* (Tel Aviv: Hakibbutz Hameuchad, 1973), p. 100. Unless otherwise noted, all translations are mine.

6   See R. W. Hamilton, "Who Built Khirbat Al Mafjar?," *Levant: Journal of the British School of Archeology in Jerusalem* 1 (1969): 61–68.

7   Noah Stern's journals, along with the court proceedings, are filed in the Hebrew Writers Association Gnazim Archive in Tel Aviv.

8   Hamilton, "Who Built Khirbat Al Mafjar?," p. 61.

9   Stern's poetry was championed in the sixties by the essayist Shlomo Grodzensky. Born, like Stern, in Lithuania, Grodzensky immigrated when thirteen with his family to New York City in 1917. He wrote for the Yiddish Weekly *Yiddisher Kempfer* until moving to Israel in 1950. For the next twenty years Grodzensky, now writing in Hebrew, would be largely responsible for drawing the reading public's attention to Anglo-American modernism and the influence of its "concentrated sobriety" on a new generation of Israeli poets, in which he saw Stern as a major forerunner. See: Shlomo Grodzensky, *Autobiography of a Reader* [Hebrew] (Tel Aviv: Hakibbutz Hameuchad, 1974), pp. 120–32.

10 Stern, *Ben Arphelim*, p. 93.

11 Hamilton, "Who Built Khirbat Al Mafjar?," p. 61.

12 Adapted from James B. Pritchard, ed., *Ancient Near Eastern Texts Relating to the Old Testament* (Princeton, NJ: Princeton University Press, 1955), p. 321.

13 Hamilton, "Who Built Khirbat Al Mafjar?," p. 65.

14 Noah Stern, "Stopgap Letter," in *Fourteen Israeli Poets: A Selection of Modern Hebrew Poetry*, ed. Dennis Silk (London: Andre Deutsch, 1976), p. 69.

15 Ibid., p. 68.

16 Adapted from R. A. Nicholson, *A Literary History of the Arabs* (Cambridge: Cambridge University Press, 1976), p. 206.

17 Cited in Hamilton, "Who Built Khirbat Al Mafjar?," p. 67.

18 Oleg Grabar, *The Formation of Islamic Art* (New Haven, CT: Yale University Press, 1987), p. 189.

19 H. B. Tristram, *The Survey of Western Palestine: The Fauna and Flora of Palestine* (London: Committe of the Palestine Exploration Find, 1884), p. 74; cited in Barbara Kreiger, *The Dead Sea: Myth, History, and Politics* (Hanover, NH: University Press of New England / Brandeis University Press, 1997), p. 79.

CHAPTER THREE

1   See William Wordsworth, *The Prelude* (text of 1805), ed. Ernest De Selincourt (London: Oxford University Press, 1960), book 5, lines 50–165.

2   See *The Works of Sir William Jones*, vol. 4 (London: Printed for G. G. and J. Robinson, Pater-Noster-Row; and R. H. Evans, 1799), p. 249.

3   Desmond O'Grady, *The Seven Arab Odes* (London: Agenda Editions, 1990), p. 13.

4   Tarafa, in *The Seven Odes*, trans. A. J. Arberry (London: Macmillan, 1957), p. 147.

5   Zuhayr, in ibid., p. 114.

6   Jacques Berque, *Cultural Expression in Arab Society Today*, trans. Robert W. Stookey (Austin: University of Texas Press, 1978), p. 125.

7   Jaroslav Stetkevych, "Name and Epithet: The Philology and Semiotics of Animal Nomenclature in Early Arabic Poetry," *Journal of Near Eastern Studies* 45, no. 2 (April 1986): 112.

8   O'Grady, *The Seven Arab Odes*, pp. 34–35.

9   For a similar view of the colocynth, its bitter taste and strange powers, see II Kings 4:38–42, in which Elisha saves the sons of the prophets of Gilgal from food poisoning ("O man of God, there is death in the pot") after wild gourds—identified as colocynth by Henry Baker Tristram on one of his expeditions to the Dead Sea in the 1860s—are shredded and mixed into pottage.

10 O'Grady, *The Seven Arab Odes*, p. 13.

11 Cited in ibid., p. 11.

12 Ezra Pound, *Literary Essays* (New York: New Directions, 1968), p. 95.

13 Gabriel Levin, *The Maltese Dreambook* (London: Anvil, 2008), p. 53.

14 Ibid., pp. 54–55.

15 A. S. Tritton, "Shir," in *The Encyclopaedia of Islam*, ed. M. Th. Houtsma et al., vol. 4 (Leiden: Brill, 1934), p. 374.

16 Pierre Reverdy, *Selected Poems*, trans. Kenneth Rexroth (London: Jonathan Cape, 1973), p. 8.

17 See *The Works of Sir William Jones*, 4:527–48.

18 Labid, in *Desert Tracings: Six Classic Arabian Odes, by Alqama, Shanfara, Labid, Antara, Al-Asha, and Dhu al-Rumma*, trans. and introduced by Michael A. Sells (Middletown, CT: Wesleyan University Press, 1989), p. 35.

19 Imru al-Qays, in Arberry, *The Seven Odes*, p. 61.

20 Adnan Haydar, "The Mu'allaqa of Imru al-Qays: Its Structure and Meaning, I," *Edebiyat* 2, no. 2 (1977): 238–39.

21 *The Works of Sir William Jones*, 4:533.

22 Irfan Shahid, "Pre-Islamic Arabia," in *The Cambridge History of Islam*, ed. P. M. Holt, Ann K. S. Lambton, and Bernard Lewis (Cambridge: Cambridge University Press, 1970), 1:17.

23 Cited in Adonis, *An Introduction to Arab Poetics*, trans. Catherine Cobham (Austin: University of Texas Press, 1990), p. 56.

24 Antara, in Arberry, *The Seven Odes*, p. 179.

25 Tarafa, in ibid., p. 84.

26 D. M. Doughty, *Passages from Arabia Deserta* (London: Penguin Travel Library, 1983), p. 3.

27 See F. U. Winnett and W. L. Reed, eds., *Ancient Records from North Arabia* (Toronto: University Of Toronto Press, 1970).

28 My translation from the French, in Ét. Coube, J. Sauvaget, and G. Wiet, eds., *Répertoire chronologique d'épigraphie Arabe* (Le Caire: Imprimerie de l'Institut Française d'archeologie orientale, 1931), 1:1–2.

29 O'Grady, *The Seven Arab Odes*, p. 18.

30 Michael Sells, "The Mu'allaqa of Tarafa," *Journal of Arabic Literature* 17 (1986): 21–33.

31 Ibid., p. 26.

32 "They wash their babies in camel-urine, and think thus to help them from insects: it is acrid, especially when the cattle have browsed of certain alkaline bushes, as the rimth. And in this water they all comb their long hair, both men and women, yet sometimes thereby bleaching their locks, so that I have seen young men's braided 'horns' grizzled." Doughty, *Passages from Arabia Deserta*, p. 66.

33 Labid, in Arberry, *The Seven Odes*, p. 147.

34 Sells, "The Mu'allaqa of Tarafa," p. 31.

35 Ibid., p. 23.

36 Ibid., p. 77.

37 *The Works of Sir William Jones*, pp. 280–81.

38 Labid, in Arberry, *The Seven Odes*, p. 23.

39 Ibid., pp. 146–47.

40 Sells, *Desert Tracings*, p. 54.

41 Ibid., p. 55.

42 Ibid.

43 Gustave E. von Grunebaum, "Growth and Structure of Arabic Poetry, A.D. 500–1000," in *The Arab Heritage*, ed. Nabih Amin Faris (Princeton, NJ: Princeton University Press, 1944), p. 129.

44 Joseph Yahalom has argued persuasively that Yehuda Halevi's most celebrated poem, "Zion, Won't You Ask," adopted by the Ashkenazi synagogue as a *kinnah*, or dirge, sung on the Ninth of Av—mourning the destruction of the Temple—was originally written as an amatory poem (*qasida*) of longing: "Like the lover of the Arabian deserts who wanders sorrowful and weeping among the abandoned dwellings of the tribal encampment of the beloved, saturated with the memory of past loves, so too our poet wanders off in his mind's eye to sites that lie at the root of the nation's conscience and of God's revelation to His prophets." Halevi's ode was further appropriated in the late nineteenth century by the Zionist movement, which saw in Halevi's longing for an ancestral homeland the prototype of its own national aspirations. See Joseph Yahalom, *Yehuda Halevi: Poetry and Pilgrimage*, trans. Gabriel Levin (Jerusalem: Magnes Press, 2009), p. 1.

45 Manuchehri, cited in "The Translations and Adaptations of Basil Bunting," by Sister Victoria Marie Forde, SC, in *Basil Bunting: Man and Poet*, ed. Carroll F. Terrell (Orono, ME: National Poetry Foundation, 1980), p. 322.

CHAPTER FOUR

1 W. M. Flinders-Petrie, "Journals," *Palestine Exploration Fund Quarterly* (1890): 227.

2   Moshe Dayan, quoted in an interview in the daily newspaper *Ha'aretz*, 13 July, 1963.

3   Daniel 4:33.

4   See Benny Morris, *Israel's Border Wars, 1949–56: Arab Infiltrators, Israeli Retaliation and the Countdown to the Suez War* (Oxford: Clarendon Press, 1993).

5   Quoted in Mitchell Ginsburg, "A Bedouin Powder Keg in the Negev," *Jerusalem Report*, September 8, 2003, p. 10.

6   Clinton Bailey, *Bedouin Poetry from Sinai and the Negev* (London: Saqi Books, 2002), pp. 362–63.

7   In 2007, a little over a year after my visits to Attir, Suleiman and his son Yahya reached an agreement with the *minhelet* and moved to Hura. Each received a large plot of land and financial assistance in building their new, two-story stone homes. Suleiman's efforts to open a shoe store were short-lived, and he soon returned to raising sheep in a large, new sheep pen he has built on his land. But the fate of Attir and the straggle of unrecognized villages along the road between Hura and the Green Line remain unclear. In 2008 it appeared that most of the villages would be officially recognized consequent to the recommendations made by the Goldberg Commission, set up during the Ulmert administration. During the summer of 2011, however, under the directive of Benjamin Netanyahu's cabinet, the commission's recommendations were reexamined and a new plan—the Prawer Plan—developed which proposes to transfer one-third of the population of the unrecognized villages (30,000 Bedouin) to Negev townships. Fiercely contested by the Regional Council of Unrecognized Bedouin Villages and by human rights organizations in Israel, the Prawer Plan has yet to be implemented.

CHAPTER FIVE

1   Franz Kafka, *The Complete Stories*, trans. Willa and Edwin Muir (New York: Schocken Books, 1976), p. 363.

2   Heraclitus, *Fragments, A Text and Translation with a Commentary*, trans. T. M. Robinson (Toronto: University of Toronto Press, 1987), fragment 48.

3   T. E. Lawrence, *Seven Pillars of Wisdom* (London: Penguin, 1963), p. 364.

4   For a full account see Taha Muhammad Ali, *So What: New and Selected Poems, 1971–2005*, trans. Peter Cole, Gabriel Levin, and Yahya Hijazi (Port Townsend, WA: Copper Canyon Press, 2006), pp. x–xii.

5   Jorge Luis Borges, "Averroes' Search," in *Collected Fictions*, trans. Andrew Hurley (London: Penguin, 1998), p. 240.

6   Avot Yeshurun, *Kol Shirav* [Collected Poems], vol. 1 (Tel Aviv: Hakibbutz Hameuchad, 1995), p. 16; my translation.

7   Aref el-Aref, *Bedouin Love, Law, and Legend*, in collaboration with Harold W. Tilley (Jerusalem: Cosmos Publishing, 1944), p. 168.

8   Yeshurun, *Kol Shirav*, p. 31.

9   Victor Segalen, *Équipée: Voyage au Pays de Réel* (Paris: Gallimard, 1983), p. 14.

10 Labid, quoted in *The Seven Odes*, trans. A. J. Arberry (London: Macmillan, 1957), p. 142.

11 Tarafa, quoted in ibid., p. 83.

12 Paul Celan, "The Meridian," in *Collected Prose*, trans. Rosmarie Waldrop (New York: Sheep Meadow Press, 1986), p. 49.

13 Yeshurun, *Kol Shirav*, p. 31; my translation.

14 Genesis 27:22.

15 Antara, in Arberry, *The Seven Odes*, p. 183. See also *Desert Tracings: Six Classic Arabian Odes, by Alqama, Shanfara, Labid, Antara, Al-Asha, and Dhu al-Rumma*, trans. and introduced by Michael A. Sells (Middletown, CT: Wesleyan University Press, 1989), p. 55. For the English reader, the stallion's mute appeal resonates in the gap between "he would have spoken to me" and Sells's suggestive "he would have let me know."

16 Zuhayr, in Arberry, *The Seven Odes*, p. 114.

17 Song of Songs 3:6.

18 This and subsequent lines from "The Dead of the Desert" translated by L. V. Snowman in Chaim Nachman Bialik, *Poems from the Hebrew*, ed. Snowman (London: Hasefer, 1924), pp. 103, 101.

19 *Diodorus of Sicily*, trans. C. H. Oldfather, Loeb Classical Library (Cambridge, MA: Harvard University Press, 1967), vol. 2, bk. 2, chap. 48, p. 41.

20 C. M. Doughty, *Passages from Arabia Deserta* (Middlesex: Penguin, Books, 1983), p. 39.

21 Herman Melville, *Clarel* (Evanston, IL: Northwestern University Press; Chicago: Newberry Library, 1991), 12:235.

22 *The Geography of Strabo*, trans. Horace Leonard Jones, Loeb Classical Library (Cambridge, MA: Harvard University Press, 1966), vol. 7, bk. 16, chap. 4, sec. 26, pp. 367–68.

23 John Milton, *Paradise Lost* (London Everyman's Library, 1929), bk. 12, line 3, p. 255.

24 Gabriel Levin, *The Maltese Dreambook* (London: Anvil, 2008), p. 56.

25 Sells, *Desert Tracings*, p. 26.

26 *The Book of Strangers: Mediaeval Arabic Graffiti on the Theme of Nostalgia*, attributed to Abu 1-Faraj al-Isfahani, trans. P. Crone and S. Moreh (Princeton, NJ: Markus Wiener, 2000), p. 79: "He said: an inscription engraved on a rock was found in the environs of the abode of Thamud, and it was translated as follows, 'O son of man, how you wrong yourself! Why don't you consider the remains of the ancients, or the end of those who received warnings, and learn a lesson and restrain yourself?' Underneath was written in Arabic handwriting, 'Indeed, thus one should do.' So it was known that fate had brought some traveler, stranger, and wanderer to this place and that he had responded with feelings of suffering."

27 *The Wisdom of the Zohar: An Anthology of Texts*, trans. David Goldstein, with introductions and explanations by Isaiah Tishby (Oxford: The Littman Library and Oxford University Press, 1991), p. 1055.

28   *The Koran Interpreted*, trans. A. J. Arberry (New York: Touchstone, 1996),
      surāh 26, *The Poets*, line 156.
29   For the full text, in Hebrew, of *Sefer Yetzirah* (Book of Creation), see Yehuda
      Liebes, *Ars Poetica in Sefer Yitzirah* (Tel Aviv: Schocken, 2000).
30   Imru al-Qays, in Arberry, *The Seven Odes*, p. 62.
31   Stern, *Ben Arphelim*, p. 93.

CHAPTER SIX

1   From *The Poems of Meleager*, verse trans. Peter Whigham, introduction
      and literal trans. Peter Jay (Berkeley: University of California Press, 1975),
      unpaginated. Jay translation Number 58.
2   Ibid., Number 2. Translation © Peter Jay, 1975.
3   Ibid., from Peter Jay's translation Number 36.
4   *Diogenes Laertius*, trans. R. D. Hicks, Loeb Classical Library (Cambridge,
      MA: Harvard University Press, 1931), vol. 2, bk. 6, chap. 8, p. 104.
5   *7 Greeks*, trans. Guy Davenport (New York: New Directions, 1995), p. 17.
6   Hicks, *Diogenes Laertius*, vol. 2, bk. 6, chap. 2, p. 43.
7   Davenport, *7 Greeks*, p. 16.
8   Ibid., p. 172.
9   "Hellenism," writes Mandelstam in "On the Nature of the Word," "is the
      conscious surrounding of man with domestic utensils instead of impersonal
      objects; the transformation of impersonal objects into domestic untensils,
      and the humanizing and warming of the surrounding world with the most
      delicate teleological warmth. Hellenism is any kind of stove near which a
      man sits, treasuring its heat as something akin to his own internal body heat."
      In *Osip Mandelstam: Complete Critical Prose*, ed. Jane Gary Harris, trans.
      Jane Gary Harris and Constance Link (Dana Point, CA: Ardis Publishers,
      1997), p. 80.
10   *Diodorus of Sicily*, trans. M. Geer Russel, Loeb Classical Library (Cambridge,
      MA: Harvard University Press, 1962), vol. 10, bk. 19, chap. 94, p. 91.
11   From "Sculptor of Tyana," in C. P. Cavafy, *Collected Poems*, trans. Edmund
      Keeley and Philip Sherrard (London: Hogarth Press, 1984), p. 26.
12   William Francis Lynch, cited in Barbara Kreiger, *The Dead Sea: Myth,
      History, and Politics* (Hanover, NH: University Press of New England /
      Brandeis University Press, 1997), pp. 65–66.
13   George Seferis, *On The Greek Style: Selected Essays on Poetry and Hellenism*,
      trans. Rex Warner and Th. D. Frangopoulos (Athens: Denise Harfey, 1966),
      p. 152.
14   Whigham and Jay, *The Poems of Meleager*; Jay translation Number 57.
15   From Meleager, *The Greek Anthology*, trans. W. R. Paton, Loeb Classical
      Library (Cambridge, MA: Harvard University Press, 1969), vol. 1, bk. 5,
      poem 160, p. 205.
16   Ibid., vol. 2, bk. 7, poem 417, p. 225.
17   Whigham and Jay, *The Poems of Meleager*, appendix.

18 Ibid.

19 Henry David Thoreau, *The Natural History Essays* (Salt Lake City: Peregrine Smith Books, 1980), p. 98.

20 Judith Green and Yoram Tsafrir, "Greek Inscriptions from Hammat Gader: A Poem by the Empress Eudocia," *Israel Exploration Journal* 32, nos. 2–3 (1982): 80. Used by permission.

21 Porphyry, *On The Cave of the Nymphs*, trans. and introductory essay Robert Lamberton (Barrytown, NY: Station Hill Press, 1983), p. 29.

22 M. D. Usher, *Homeric Stitchings: The Homeric Centos of the Empress Eudocia* (Lanham, MD: Rowman and Littlefield, 1998), p. 13.

23 Cited in Kenneth G. Holum, *Theodosian Empresses: Women and Imperial Dominion in Antiquity* (Berkeley: University of California Press, 1982), p. 221.

24 Cited in Usher, *Homeric Stitchings*, p. 1.

25 Eunapius, "Lives of the Philosophers," in *Philostratus and Eunapius, The Lives of the Sophists*, ed. W. C. Wright, series 134 (Cambridge, MA: Harvard University Press, 1921), pp. 362–72; quotation is from p. 369.

26 Green and Tsafrir, "Greek Inscriptions from Hammat Gader," p. 95.

27 Meleager, *The Greek Anthology*, vol. 1, bk. 1, poem 105, pp. 44–45.

28 Dennis Silk, "Tryphon," *Encounter*, December 1969, p. 15.

29 E. L. Sukenik, "The Ancient Synagogue of El-Hammeh," *Journal of the Palestine Oriental Society* 15 (1935): 125–26.